UNCOMMON DUTIES IN THE UNITED STATES AIR FORCE

Col. (Ret.) Marty Z. Khan, EdD

Copyright © 2022 Col. (Ret.) Marty Z. Khan, EdD
All rights reserved
First Edition

PAGE PUBLISHING
Conneaut Lake, PA

First originally published by Page Publishing 2022

The views expressed in this publication are those of the author and do not necessarily reflect the official policy or position of the Department of Defense or the US government. No classified material was used to write this book or referenced in this book. The Department of Defense cleared this book for publication.

ISBN 978-1-6624-6275-7 (pbk)
ISBN 978-1-6624-6276-4 (digital)

Printed in the United States of America

CONTENTS

Acknowledgment 7
The Author 9
Introduction: The Context 13

Part I 19
    The Selective Service's Draft Board and Me 19
    Enlistment and Basic Training: The Beginning 21
    Reflections on Substantive Assignments 30
    Reflections on professional military education 52

Part II 57
    Introduction 57
    Reflections on Leadership 60
    Reflections on Succeeding in the Mission 88
    On Success 90

Part III 108
    Introspective Thoughts on the United States Air
        Force Culture 108
    Introspective Thoughts on the Future and Challenges 114
    Concluding Remarks 117

With honor and humility, I dedicate this book to all American servicemen and women, especially airmen, whose duty made the reunification of Germany possible. This was a significant event in my military career, one that I thought was impossible because of the numerous military exercises I participated in West Germany on exploring possibilities to stop the Soviet Union's army from marching over and occupying the country.

In the first week of November 1989, I was in West Berlin for a few days, representing the Department of Defense. After dinner, my colleague and I headed back to our hotel, but we soon noticed multitudes of all sorts of people walking in the direction of the Berlin Wall. We knew that there were demonstrations in Eastern Germany[1] and that the situation in East Berlin was tense. We followed the throngs. Not long afterward, we were near the Reichstag building. The crowds were thicker, and soon, I noticed a few white crosses. I paused and read the words, memorializing East Germans, killed trying to escape to West Berlin to live free. At the wall, I noticed many young people sitting and standing on top of it, celebrating, and many others were hammering with all their might and enthusiasm to crack open passageway to freedom and for pieces of souvenirs. I looked through a few cracked areas and saw several East German border police trying to push and prevent East Germans from walking over to West Berlin.

The East German Communist regime was collapsing. I thought of Presidents John Kennedy and Ronald Reagan and all those airmen and other Americans who participated in the Berlin Airlift to save the city from starvation by the Soviet Union. It was through this enduring support from the United States that Germany's unification

---

[1] Deutsche Demokratische Republik (DDR).

became possible. After many duty assignments in Western Germany, I never thought that the Berlin Wall would fall in my lifetime. In West Germany, I participated in countless exercises to explore scenarios on how to maintain West Germany's territorial integrity from an invading army. And when the wall fell, it was a momentous event for those US personnel serving in Germany at the time. I was a witness to this event, and a piece of the Berlin Wall, which I purchased from some entrepreneurial children in West Berlin on November 8, 1989, now rests in my home. It serves as a reminder of the East Germans' struggle for freedom and the subsequent and rightful reunification of Germany. The United States Air Force personnel through decades of service made that freedom a possibility. My first overseas assignment was at Rhein-Main Air Force Base, outside of Frankfurt, Germany, in 1978; and my last assignment at the time of retirement in 2015 was at Ramstein Air Force Base. And through many assignments in Germany, the fall of the Berlin Wall, along with the collapse of communism in East Germany, was a significant point in my air force career. But more importantly, the duty in Germany and elsewhere resulted in numerous enduring friendships with Germans, Danes, Dutch, French, Italians, and Spanish, which I continue to hold dear.

Additionally, I dedicate my book to my training instructors (Sergeants N. E. Whitmer and W. R. Copp), who enthusiastically welcomed me and subsequently guided me through my basic training at Lackland Air Force Base, San Antonio, Texas, while I was assigned to 3703 Training Squadron, Flight 17; all my military superiors (officers and noncommissioned officers), in January–February 1976; Department of Defense colleagues to include civilians, who supported and mentored me early in my service; and everyone at the Air Force Reserve Personnel Center in Denver, Colorado, who responded to every question I had relating to my career.

ACKNOWLEDGMENT

Serving in the world's greatest air force was an honor. I am very grateful for the privilege to serve, and without any unfavorable incident, that impacted my career, from start to retirement. The US Air Force took me to many countries for duty, and each assignment shaped my life, professionally and personally. My professional career took a trajectory I never had imagined. Each assignment resulted in broadening my perspectives and worldview and made new friends in the United States and overseas and all for the good.

As an airman, I represented the United States in several delegations overseas to work on strengthening the US partnership with allies. My narration is about some aspects of substantive issues, relating to the president's national security strategy,[2] with a focus on leadership attributes, and what it took to achieve mission success. I will conclude with a note on challenges ahead for the air force.

Using some vignettes, I will highlight some of my associations with fellow airmen and international officers to achieve the issues of vital importance to the United States. These descriptions will give insight into what I thought made it possible for me to be successful to accomplish the mission for all my air force assignments.

In appreciation, I would like to extend my sincere thanks to my wife, Rebecca Stein Handele, a willing and a proud wingman, during my Air Force Reserve career. Her support to me during my worldwide assignments kept the situation on the home front (in Florida) always under control. Knowing she was there gave me the assurance there was no need to worry about the numerous things to do, especially during the yearly hurricane seasons. It was her encouragement

---

[2] The president's vision on how the US Government will protect the security of the United States, its values, institutions, and overseas interests.

and support that enabled me to complete this book to convey a message on what I learned during my assignments to current and future airmen. I also wish to thank my parents and my family for their encouragement when I decided to join the air force and their continued support during all my active and reserve assignments.

With deep respect, I would like to acknowledge my sincere thanks to one of my former professors, Dr. Aline Stomfay-Stitz, in my doctoral program. She was a very special friend, and she encouraged me years ago to write this book, offering many kind words of support. Writing about my working experiences, as she had said numerous times, would be an immense opportunity to share my experiences with others. Aline was a brave American patriot. She, too, served the United States, during the Cold War, in Europe, with a critical mission to spread the word of freedom and hope to East Europeans living behind the Iron Curtain, especially those, in Soviet-occupied Hungary.

Lastly, numerous individuals who I worked with had to some degree helped me to achieve the rank of colonel. Here are some of those individuals: Vice Admiral Michael Franken, Brig. Gen. Joseph Shaefer, Rear Admiral Martha Herb, Colonels Andy Cox, Elio Castellano, Gordon Hendrickson, Giles Light, Charles MacDonald, Chris Moffett, Tom Nickerson, Mike Ryan, Greg Winston, and Vernon Vandiver.

THE AUTHOR

I am probably one of the last groups of American men to be selected to report for induction processing. I registered for the draft as required in March 1971 and received the 1A classification (available for military service), during a very difficult time in the United States, while the Vietnam War was still raging. Common during this time were demonstrations on college campuses, where some students would proudly burn their draft cards. I never did.

While in college, I petitioned my draft board for exemption because I was a college student and the only son in my family. The draft board denied my request. In February 1972, the draft numbers were announced, and my number was low enough to report for induction processing. Not long afterward, the draft board notified me to take the required aptitude tests and medical examination in New York City, as a result of receiving a low number in the draft. President Richard Nixon ended the draft on January 27, 1973, which was a monumental decision that impacted every young man's life and future in the United States. For me, personally, I did not have to report for military duty. While American servicemen casualties in the Vietnam War were increasing, there were positive hopes of the war coming to an end, as negotiations between the United States and North Vietnam intensified, with a peace treaty in the works.

I enlisted in the US Air Force in 1976.[3] In 1978, I transferred into the Air Force Reserve, and after attaining the rank of technical sergeant,

---

[3] As one who was born into the Muslim faith, I never felt any personal religious conflicts joining the United States Air Force. My religion was always a personal matter when I first enlisted and still is today. I suppose the first event that involved issues of the Muslim faith during my membership in the US Air Force was the overthrow of the Shah of Iran and the emergence of Ayatollah Khomeini as a key political leader in Iran. At that time, there was much discussion between my

I earned my commission on July 31, 1987, as a second lieutenant, and I began my training to be an intelligence officer. In April 2000, after serving with several Air Force Reserve organizations, I was charged with assisting the US military representative (a three-star general officer), in Brussels, Belgium, in matters relating to integrating US policy into the North Atlantic Treaty Organization (NATO) plans at the strategic level. I also supported the Defense Attaché System, the Joint Interagency Task Force (East), and with both defense advisors the US Mission to NATO and to the European Union, respectively.

In 2006, the United Air Force Reserve Command selected a handful of reservists to attend the in-residence Air War College program, at Maxwell Air Force Base in Montgomery, Alabama. I was one of those, and I completed my program in the class 2008, with a master of strategic studies.

From June 2008 to July 2009, I was deployed to serve as the country director at Headquarters, Central Command (CENTCOM), MacDill Air Force Base, Tampa, Florida, responsible for all aspects of CENTCOM's security cooperation programs with Pakistan. I traveled several times to Pakistan and India with military leaders from Central Command and Pacific Command (including Generals Martin Dempsey and David Petraeus) to deepen US partnership

---

military colleagues on the issues of Muslim radicalism in the world. I never felt uncomfortable with the discussions. All my air force colleagues treated me with the utmost respect, who knew I was a Muslim—in fact, very few of them knew. I suppose, more importantly, in many meetings involving strategy and policy with air force leaders that I attended, I never heard any disparaging remarks about the Muslim faith. In fact, the leaders conducted themselves in the most professional manner and with military decorum. It was in such meetings that I came to realize that the US Air Force and its culture were truly professional and one with which I would be proud to continue to associate. After the horrific terrorist attacks on September 11, 2001, which involved Muslims with an extremely bizarre radical Muslim ideology, it was even more important to me, as an American, to continue serving. I never did nor did I have any personal philosophical conflicts on whether to serve in the fight against extremists, who use the Islamic faith to plan attacks against the United States. Interacting with Americans of all faiths and attending services in their respective places of worship made me, in my opinion, a more understanding person.

engagements with both countries and also regional peace through collaboration.

On May 1, 2012, I was selected for promotion to colonel.[4] The US Air Force Reserve Command assigned me as the intelligence mobilization augmentee to the US Air Forces, Europe and Africa, at Ramstein Air Force Base in Germany. It was indeed a coincidence that as a second lieutenant, I was assigned to a reserve unit at Ramstein and as a colonel, too.

I participated in military exercises in Belgium, Germany, Greece, Korea, Qatar, and Turkey. I was a member of US military delegations to Armenia, Azerbaijan, India, Pakistan, and The Republic of Georgia, and frequently, worked alongside marines, sailors and soldiers, and coast guard members, in the United States and overseas. I retired on February 22, 2015, at Ramstein Air Force Base, Germany.[5]

In my civilian capacity, I worked with the Defense Intelligence Agency, as an intelligence officer, and served in the United Kingdom, Afghanistan, and Germany. I have a doctorate in educational leadership and authored *Access to Higher Education: Leadership Challenges in Florida and South Africa*[6]. I am a life member of the Air Force Association, Veterans of Foreign Wars, and the Naval War College Foundation.

---

[4] After promotion, I had the opportunity to serve on a reserve promotions board. It was a very humble experience to be part of a team to review lieutenant colonels' promotion packages and select who should be promoted to colonel.

[5] My complete award and decoration packet: Defense Superior Service Medal, Defense Meritorious Service Medal with two oak leaf clusters, Meritorious Service Medal, Joint Service Commendation Medal, Air Force Commendation Medal with one oak leaf cluster, Joint Service Achievement Medal, Joint Meritorious Unit Award, Air Force Organizational Excellence Award with one oak leaf cluster, Air Reserve Forces Meritorious Service Medal with two bronze oak leaf clusters, National Defense Service Medal with bronze star, Global War on Terrorism Service Medal, Air and Space Campaign Medal, Air Force Longevity Service Award with one silver and one bronze oak leaf clusters, Armed Forces Reserve Medal with "M" Device and Silver Hourglass, and Air Force Training Ribbon with one oak leaf cluster. Awarded the Joint Chiefs of Staff Badge.

[6] *Access to Higher Education: Leadership Challenges in Florida and South Africa.* Lanham, MD: University Press of America, 2005.

INTRODUCTION

The Context

This book is the introspection of my service in the US Air Force. I will focus on what I learned and elaborate on what it took to be a successful airman. I will conclude with some perspectives on the challenges ahead. It is my hope this personal narrative has broader applications especially for airmen and other members of the armed services to use in their professional careers and enable them to be effective in accomplishing their respective mission.

I will highlight a number of key aspects of my career to provide some contextual framework on how airmen contribute to policy making, relating to national security issues. Also, I will share some vignettes of my experiences on the dynamics of how military leaders lead. For example, my years of duty at Headquarters, Central Command, and the years at the United States Military Delegation to the North Atlantic Treaty Organization (NATO) as a reservist were truly superb assignments that gave me the opportunity to work on critical national and geopolitical security issues. I worked with leaders (general officers, ambassadors, and senior ranking civilians) from every branch of the armed services (including the Coast Guard), colleagues in the Joint Chiefs of Staff, Office of the Secretary of Defense, and the Department of State involving issues of vital importance to the United States. These experiences gave me a rich and profound understanding of the dynamics to make US policy and why. Moreover, it gave me a deeper appreciation for the United States, its founding values, and democratic institutions.

I hope that my book will add one more voice to the numerous collections of life experiences by patriots on leadership in the

US Air Force. Different perspectives are important to learn about how individuals solved their problems in conditions that one may or may not experience. How individuals, especially low-ranking ones, manage tasks in complex organizations and take action even during life-threatening instances of adversity is also important to understand.[7] My story adds another voice and perspective to those who have already told their personal stories, serving the United States, in different work assignments.

During my association with the air force, I served voluntarily. I had the freedom to terminate my service at any time, if I had so desired. I decided to serve because I wanted to. For three decades (without any break in service and having maintained all security credentials and authorizations), I served because of my belief in the air force mission, and more importantly, I enjoyed what I did. I always knew that somehow in my own way and yes, despite my rank, I, too, was contributing to helping maintain peace and freedom in the United States and in many areas of the world.

From the very start of my enlistment in 1976 to earning my commission in 1987 and onward, I have had extraordinary opportunities to participate and contribute my ideas on a variety of military issues vital to protect the United States' overseas interests. The issues ranged from air force functional career jobs (communication, transportation, intelligence, and security cooperation to support the war on terror) to keep air force pilots prepared for worldwide deployments and to engage with foreign partners in complex security programs, valued at hundreds of millions of dollars.

The experiences I gained were critical to shaping my air force life. Additionally, it reinforced my philosophical beliefs of what the

---

[7] For three perspectives from two amazing marines and one soldier about their combat experiences in Afghanistan and Iraq, read the following:
Nathaniel C. Fick, *One Bullet Away: The Making of A Marine Officer* (New York: Houghton Mifflin Harcourt, 2006).
Wesley Gray, *Embedded: A Marine Corps Advisor Inside the Iraqi Army* (Annapolis, Maryland: Naval Institute Press, 2009).
Craig M. Mullaney, *The Unforgiving Minute: A Soldier's Education* (New York: The Penguin Press, 2009).

United States stood for, what freedom meant to me, and why freedom must be protected. As just an ordinary unpretentious airman, I never sought any recognition for doing what I did. I was expected to do my job, and I did just that. I expected nothing more and wanted no special recognition. For me, the privilege of serving was enough.

As a loyal airman, duty was in a system, an organization, with a mission that was critical. Critical here was the necessity of a strong team to execute the mission. There was really no expectation for recognition, and such belief would not have been in the best traditions and culture of the air force. The numerous awards and decorations I received over the years have the narrative describing my accomplishments and were only possible with the support of leaders who did the right things to train and shape their teams to accomplish the organization's mission.

In my career, a broad range of opportunities always seemed to be accessible to me. I do not believe it was luck or being in the right place at the right time. It was, I believe, was my desire to perform my duty and always focus on the mission. My continuous training and my personal professional self-development provided me the foundations for new opportunities and the confidence my superiors had in me. It was indeed my air force training that gave me grounding, the background knowledge, and the confidence necessary to execute my mission anytime and in any place in the world.

I worked on a variety of strategic policy matters with colleagues from various organizations (military and civilian). These assignments presented me with opportunities to work on issues that were of major importance to our elected leaders, military, and civilian policy makers. Moreover, I worked on issues involving humanitarian projects for internally displaced persons in Pakistan, interacted with European Union officials on the refugee situation in the Darfur (Sudan), supported the US team for the Intermediate-Range Nuclear Forces Treaty (INF Treaty), monitored and directed some aspects of security cooperation projects to strengthen military-to-military capabilities between the United States and Pakistan, and helped to develop strategy and national policy issues at the United States Mission to NATO, the European Union, and at the United States Military Delegation to

NATO's Military Committee on various complex policy and security cooperation issues.

In addition, I had the privilege to work with some very brilliant and dedicated officers at Central Command on issues relating to the US/Pakistan partnership and planning various degrees of strategy in the war on terror against the terrorists along the Afghanistan/Pakistan border. Also, I interacted with officers from forty-four countries[8] during my in-residence Air War College Program in Montgomery, Alabama, which was an astounding opportunity to listen and learn what those officers think about the United States.

My involvement with military activities over the years has given me unique opportunities to see how effective and *not so effective* leaders tackle complex problems, many of which have a direct impact on the United States' foreign policy interests and the security of the homeland. Through my observations and firsthand experiences, I became more convinced that effective leaders seem to have unique skills to lead people and achieve their respective organization's mission. It is through certain unique skills such as instinctive intuition, solid background knowledge in many functional areas, and abilities to communicate and listen to people from different backgrounds, think quickly, and judge others that they seem to confidently make tough decisions. Equally important, through my observations, I am also convinced that leaders seem to project themselves in a very positive and respectful manner and, always, with friendly eye contact. From such individuals, I learned why it is important to make decisions that are in the best interest of the country and making sure that all members of the team see how he or she fits and contributes to the decisions.

On the other hand, from *not so effective* leaders, I learned what not to be. From my point of view, I believed the "distance" from the

---

[8] For example from: Algeria, Australia, Bahrain, Bangladesh, Botswana, Bulgaria, Canada, Colombia, Czech Republic, Egypt, El Salvador, France, Germany, Ghana, Greece, Honduras, India, Indonesia, Kuwait, Lithuania, Malaysia, Mexico, Morocco, Netherlands, Nigeria, Norway, Pakistan, Philippines, Poland, Qatar, Romania, Saudi Arabia, Spain, Taiwan, Tunisia, Ukraine, United Arab Emirates, and the United Kingdom.

leader and his or her team, a lack of respect for others, and the inability to show the human side of one's position that I found to be valuable learning opportunities of what I should never be. Though such leaders accomplish the mission, it generally comes with a cost, essentially, diminishing morale. It was from these *not so effective* leaders that I also learned more about myself and what I needed to be effective. Luckily, I encountered just a few of these *not so effective* leaders. That label, *not so effective*, certainly has negative connotations and implications for not only one personally but also an organization.

Self-awareness and self-critique are absolutely critical to be effective and successful. Both require honest personal introspection of oneself to determine how one must modify and change one's behavior to motivate a team. Without a personal commitment to perform introspection or even understanding the value of doing so, it is unlikely that anyone can begin to see those personal things or habits that may be necessary to change to be effective and successful.

Considering the scrutiny with which military personnel are expected to endure and which are required for some assignments, it is thus obviously critical for everyone to comply with strict fiduciary and oversight guidelines. Within the guidelines are the expectations to accomplish one's mission within standards of quality, in which peoples' lives may be at risk. As a result, one's ability to modify one's behavior to meet the established guidelines and expectation is extremely critical. Though the military's use of the autocratic style of leadership is generally common, the idea to conduct a personal introspection should be seen as a strength. The introspection process provides one with an opportunity to identify areas for improvement (or not performing to the accepted standards) only if one is willing to accept one's own weaknesses through an honest self-reflection.

And so, from this snapshot of my service, I will craft my air force story. I will share what I believe is useful information not only for air force personnel but also for those who now serve in all of the other branches of the uniformed services.

PART I

This section will focus on my initial contact with the military, my draft board. I will cover some of my key assignments, my professional military education, and describe what I learned. These experiences gave me the foundation and background knowledge to be effective on duty.

The Selective Service's Draft Board and Me

In 1971, I registered with my draft board in New York City, as required by law. I was assigned the draft category 1A (translation: available for military service and could potentially be called to military duty in a draft). The Vietnam War was seemingly out of control, and the ongoing political contacts between the United States and North Vietnam were not achieving the results for a peace settlement. Throughout the United States, the issue of being drafted was a deep concern for many young men. It was not uncommon during this time for young men to inquire in discussions about others' draft status—it was a common theme of interest during conversations, which I found within my circle of friends, asking, "What is your classification?" I believe that for the most part, most young men did not want to go to South Vietnam. I did not want to be drafted and feared, if drafted, I would most likely have to go to Vietnam. The fear of going there was a matter of enormous concern to my parents and for me, too. I knew I had to comply with the legal requirement to register for the draft and did just that.

Also, in 1971, in the fall, I enrolled as a full-time college student and worked part-time. Soon afterward and after much discussion with my parents, I decided to write a letter to my draft board to appeal the classification. I felt that if I were to be drafted, the service would interrupt my education. I wanted a change in the classification based on honest reasons. However, I had absolutely no intentions to seek a change based on contrived ideas, or as a conscientious objector, or one based on religious beliefs, which I did not. I spent many hours composing the letter to articulate my rationale (two key points: going to college and being the only son in the family) for the change of classification. It was not before long (perhaps a couple of months or so) that I heard from my draft board—my request to change my classification was denied. In 1972, despite being enrolled full-time in college and the only son in the family, I was notified to report for induction processing (I believe my draft number was 20, and thus, an absolute certainty, barring no medical issues, I would be reporting for duty). My parents were worried, and the fear of my being drafted and the possibility of going to Vietnam was undoubtedly a heavy burden for them, especially my mother. Some of my college friends who had deferments advised me to go to Canada. While I initially gave it some thought, I felt it would not be the right thing to do and that I would have never wanted the *draft dodger* label to be pinned on me.[9]

Shortly thereafter, I received my notification to report for aptitude testing, which I took at a military processing office in lower Manhattan. At the time, President Richard Nixon was faced with numerous challenges (military strategy, ongoing complex negotiations with North Vietnam, and the failure of the South Vietnamese government to increase its legitimacy throughout South Vietnam) and, more importantly, domestic political pressure in the United States to end the war. In January 1973, President Nixon ended the draft and all future calls for draftees. The order for me to report to duty ended. It brought a much relief to many, many young men and other Americans, including my parents and myself. For many others throughout the nation, the end of the draft produced a euphoria of

---

[9] A few years later after being notified of my being drafted, I found out that a high school friend of mine went to Canada to avoid the draft—he, apparently, never registered for it. For me, personally, I knew I made the right choice, a moral choice, to register and to proceed with the draft requirements.

relief across college campuses especially those who were eligible to be drafted. For me, it was a personal relief that I would not be drafted and that I could continue my college education, which I did.

After a few years of going part-time in college and working and without any focus as to what I wanted in life, I enlisted in the US Air Force, to explore opportunities, one of which was to be a pilot (but later, I was unable to meet eyesight requirements, and that goal came not to be).

Enlistment and Basic Training: The Beginning

One very cold morning in January 1976, my parents drove me to Fort Hamilton in Brooklyn, New York, without saying much along the way. After arriving at the fort, they wished me well. It was not a happy occasion for them and for me knowing that my parents did not agree with my decision to join. Saying goodbye to them was indeed difficult. I just felt that with the silence and the few words we interchanged, it was difficult for them to see me leave.

After several hours of in-processing at the fort, I departed for LaGuardia Airport in Queens, New York City, for San Antonio Municipal Airport, Texas, with a few other young men my age. Once at the airport in San Antonio, I was greeted by air force personnel who guided me along with the other young men to a bus, each with either long hair, including myself, or Afro-style hairstyles and bell-bottoms blue jeans. The bus stop, the only stop, was at Lackland Air Force Base. The initial welcome at Lackland was about nine o'clock in the evening. It appeared to me later that the timing was obviously planned to ensure all members did not have any time for socializing or sightseeing after arriving on the base.

I was assigned to the 3703 Training Squadron, Flight[10] 17, with forty other members. We were all greeted with a firm and deafening

---

[10] Flight is the smallest unit in the Air Force. Other increasing units are squadron, group, wing, and numbered Air Force. More specifically, the *Air Force Magazine* (Journal of the Air Force Association) in its 2008 USAF Almanac noted that:
> The fundamental unit of the working Air Force is the *wing*.
> The typical Air Force base is built around a wing. Some

enthusiastic welcome by our training instructors (Sergeants Whitmer and Copp) and other key leaders from the training squadron, whose roles did not mean anything to me at that time. After some administrative formalities, we were subjected to a very close-up, in-your-face, inspection outside the building where we in-processed. A cold northern wind blew and pierced our clothing (we were ordered to leave our winter jackets in the building); most of us, including me, shivered. The close-up inspection was interrupted by inspiring remarks and very profound, but not funny, statements from our training instructors—the instructors (one tall (Whitmer), and the other, the shorter one (Copp))—got the attention they wanted and were entitled to. In a quiet and solemn formation, we waited nervously, for the next order, then the next, and the next. The orders came, with intermittent pauses, and with no degree of prediction, but they came.

The review did what it was intended to do—showing who was in charge. The instructors' power and responsibility entrusted unto them to train new recruits were obvious. Almost every new recruit got a special close-up "in your face" penetrating stare and an occasional unpredictable grin from each instructor. Both instructors walked around the new recruits at a quick pace, with no logic, in different directions. They would suddenly stop and conduct an off-the-cuff, in-your-face inspection on the lucky recruit. Mine was on one hand comical (I did not think it was comical then; after graduation, this thought came to mind) and, on the other hand, was very serious.

The instructor poked his head toward me and with the brim of his hat ("Smokey the Bear" style and, essentially, the ones some state troopers wear) about one inch from my face. He stared into my eyes,

---

wings are commanded by a general officer, while others are headed by a colonel. An objective wing contains an *operations group*, which includes aircrews, intelligence units, and others; a *maintenance group*, which includes maintenance squadrons; a *support group*, which includes such functions as civil engineers, logistics readiness, and security forces; and a *medical group*. Most individual officers and Airmen are assigned to a squadron, which may be composed of several *flights*. (p. 36, May 2008)

and did not blink. He nevertheless had a slightly friendly but serious grin. I thought he looked anxious, excited, and angry. I tightened my jaws and pressed hard on my teeth and stopped breathing for a few seconds. I continued breathing, and I tried to avoid grinning. I did not dare to make eye contact. He stared at me. I did the same, but extraordinarily, I could not see his eyes even though I looked at them. I paused for a few seconds, waiting for, I believe, an unsolicited response from him. I slowly took a deep breath and kept my stance. He continued to stare and shouted a few questions at me. Trembling from the cold air and a growing fear of his concentrated stare, I answered him. He seemed satisfied. I was relieved, and I tried to breathe normally. He then moved on to the next recruit. Yes, I was scared of him, and I kept looking straight ahead for the fear he might suddenly turn around and subject me to more questions. But looking at the instructor in formation was not permissible, as we learned early that evening.

One recruit made eye contact with an instructor, and I thought at that moment, the world had ended.

The instructor shouted, "What are you looking at me for?"

Somewhat nonchalantly, the recruit (from New York—I recalled seeing him at Fort Hamilton) said, "At you?"

The instructor came closer to the recruit and then roared, "What?"

There was silence for a few seconds, and then the recruit said, "Oh man, nothing. Yea-a-ah, Yea-a-ah, man, nothing really."

There were some giggles in the group. The instructor froze in his position, paused, and then snarled, "Flight attention."

The entire group moved to an uncoordinated out of line but reinforced attention. Obviously, as new recruits, it was an uncoordinated alignment of each row like a ragtag, clueless group. But everyone stood still, which was what we thought "flight attention" meant. The formation was quiet—so quiet, I heard every step of the instructors' boots (with metal taps) hitting the concrete pad. They took a few steps and paused a few seconds, and I did not know where they were but had the fear one of them could be standing right behind me. I heard a few more steps, and the routine was repeated several times. This approach was very effective to increase every recruit's anxiety, and it reinforced the command of attention.

"Now listen up," the short instructor howled, and he seemed to project his voice at a higher pitch than the taller one. He got even more of everyone's attention—the formation was now absolutely still.

He paused for a few seconds and then shouted, "From now on, you will never have direct eye contact with us when you are in formation. Understand?"

Every recruit shouted, "Yes, sir."

The instructor howled, "I can't hear you."

That routine went on about five or six more times. He made his point. He stopped howling his orders, and then the tall instructor yelled, "Pick up your bags."

I grabbed my American Tourister suitcase. It was somewhat heavy—I was the only one with a suitcase, which was something I noticed when I got off the bus, as I struggled to keep pace with my new friends. I had packed with some casual civilian clothes (with the hopes to do some sightseeing in San Antonio) and a couple of books to read—which I never got to because there was no time for leisure reading and more importantly because all personal and nonessential items were not allowed in our possession after being moved into the dormitory.

He yelled again, "Attention."

After a few seconds or so, he said, "Put down your bags."

Everyone complied.

He yelled again, "Pick them up."

Everyone obeyed and waited fearfully for the next order.

The instructor continued the routine for another eight or nine times, and each time we held our bags, he rebuked, praised, berated, encouraged, criticized, and persuaded us to listen to him and the other instructor and do as they say every time.

To make sure we understood what he said, he yelled, "Do you understand?"

Everyone shouted, "Yes, sir."

It was quiet for a few seconds, and then the instructor shouted again, "Do you understand?"

Everyone answered but, this time, screaming, "Yes, sir." It was a recurring theme, which went on a few more times. The screaming apparently had a good effect. It basically, I believed, allowed each new recruit, including me, to release whatever anxieties we had and just place us in a semirelaxed mood. And it was at that point that I believed everyone had just had their first orientation of what it was going to be like in the air force basic training.

Understanding the instructors' role, I just had the feeling that really deep down, the instructors were serious about the trust placed on them. It was obvious their authoritarian welcome on that cold January evening was meant to be interpreted as "Trust me. I don't need your opinion. I'll transform you into an airman. Just wait and see." And they did.

Just as everyone was getting uncomfortable and tense standing, the tall instructor commanded us to stand at the *at ease*. It appeared no one knew what that was. He then explained to us what he meant and what to do with our hands. He welcomed everyone again to Lackland Air Force Base and then extended an enthusiastic invitation to us to the dining hall for our first military "midnight" breakfast, a few minutes after midnight. As I recall, one of the training instructors (the short one) stood at the head of the line. He stood there with a serious look and occasional unemotional grins as he inspected each recruit's plate and made some sarcastic remarks about the amount of food in some individuals' plates. He stared at each of us as we ordered our meals and we grabbed our plates of scrambled eggs, potatoes, gravy, and pieces of beef. Very carefully, each of us passed him, avoiding any eye contact with him. Fearfully, each walked into the dining area and nervously sat next to a colleague. We were told not to eat until permission was granted. Each of us looked at our plate, and just could not wait to eat. We waited a few seconds, and with permission granted, we devoured our food. It was not before long (it was indeed not a leisurely meal) when we left the dining hall and marched haphazardly with our belongings to our dormitory.

From the first night in the dormitory, I suddenly began to realize the monumental tasks ahead of me. Word went around quickly that if one failed to complete the course, the individual would have to repeat it. I said to myself that was not going to happen to me. I thought immediately that to be successful in the program, I would have to get along with every member of my team, especially the individual right and left of my cot. At the first opportunity, I introduced myself to classmates, one from California and the other from Utah, whose cots were left and right to my cot. That introduction and the pledge we made to help one another out were enormously beneficial as I would learn during and at the end of each day of training. It strengthened our friendship and also helped to establish the basis for maintaining a strong cohesion for the entire flight.

Very early, perhaps at 0530, we were awoken from the noise from a nightstick hitting on an aluminum garbage container cover. Suddenly, everyone jumped out of bed, shocked and in a daze. Sure enough, we were all stunned by the bright lights. We turned to the lights at the hallway door; our instructors stood at attention in freshly starched uniforms. Each had the usual wide and unfriendly grin. They got our attention and explained that the squadron commander will welcome us at 0730. I am not sure if we were excited, scared, or indifferent, but everyone just seemed to have a tremendous burst of energy and enthusiasm. We took that as an order to get ready, groomed of course, for the commander.

After breakfast, we met the squadron commander. We were told beforehand, and much emphasis was placed on the fact that he was the squadron commander, which implicitly meant we were to respect him. We were also reminded of no eye contact with him, especially when standing at attention. The squadron commander appeared. He was a major, and he seemed to be important. Indeed, he was very impressive. He walked around our group, confidently, in his air force class A (dress suit) uniform. As new recruits, still in scraggy civilian clothes, we were just awed with his presence, especially his uniform, his ribbons, and his demeanor. He immediately got everyone's respect, with his firm stance and his stare. There was no eye contact with him, not directly of course. His welcome remarks were simple and to the point. He implored us to do a good job and listen to the instructors. He told us if we had any problems, we were free to drop by his office. I seriously doubt if any recruit would have taken up his offer even though it was indeed sincere; it was perhaps just a customary and obligatory statement. After wishing us well, he departed, and all of us immediately turned our attention back to our friendly drill instructors and waited for the next order.

Both instructors kept us at attention and reminded us to always remember what the commander said. They also asked us to keep in mind we were to begin our training in which they planned to transform us into airmen and they had all intentions to succeed. My recollection from the encounter was that I was amazed by the squadron commander's presence. At that moment, I thought that I could never ever be an officer in the US Air Force. I felt I did not have what it took and could never be able to do what these impressive individuals were required to do.

For me, basic training was somewhat of a challenge. The challenge was essentially the fear of the unknown—being with forty other young men and going through a very rigorous and regimented program. However, I was determined not to fail. To succeed, I quickly began to see the instructors' mission and their point of view. I understood the instructors' motivation, and I was determined to persevere with all the academic and physical challenges ahead of me. The education lectures and written examinations I found to be very simple, but the physical exercises were difficult. Keeping up with teammates was sometimes grueling. I nevertheless kept up the pace. Despite my lack of physical conditioning then, I completed all segments of the physical program. I was never the last person to finish—neither was I ever close to being the first—and behind most of my team.

During the first week of basic training, both training instructors were very direct and sometimes to the point of projecting an assertive mindset. Considering the number of individuals in the class, from different cultural backgrounds and from various parts of the United States, the instructors had a monumental task to mold and shape forty young men into airmen.

Starting the second week, the stress level increased. The instructors' positions were, of course, sacrosanct; they received all the respect they were entitled to and sometimes a lot more. At the end of the second week, my instructors called me into their office in the dormitory and said they had selected me for a special assignment. They wanted to know if I would like to volunteer to do some administrative reports for our team, which are required to be sent on a daily basis to the squadron commander. I remembered what others in my team have said over and over again, "Never volunteer for anything!" Scared to say no, I thought for a moment, *What would this assignment entail?* Standing at attention in their offices, they both looked at me waiting for an answer. Remembering what my colleagues told me and without not knowing the challenges of the assignment, I said yes—I would accept to do the work. However, I did indeed have some degree of trepidation. I saluted them to show my respect. Looking straight at me, they cautioned me never to salute them because they were not commissioned officers. They nevertheless thanked me for agreeing to accept the assignment, and I would be called the *House Mouse*, as the position came with the call sign or name. The senior instructor said he expected me to take the responsibilities and not say no. After explaining what I needed to do, they then offered access to their offices to me to do the administrative work. So from the second week, my relationships with my training instructors changed. It became more cordial and less stressful. Now I was the *House Mouse* for my team, and I had a direct link to both instructors. Indeed, it was a position of power and influence.

Being the *House Mouse* despite the additional work in the evenings had its benefits. Essentially, I had full access to their private office in the evening—an incredible privilege and, indeed, one with a status. It was a quiet place, one to spend a few minutes each evening. The instructors told me I could use their radio anytime. I was ecstatic about the radio. Access to a private office and a radio was an incredible morale booster. Listening to music and news of the outside world (outside of basic training barracks) was a relief from the regimented life. Every evening, I would invite a couple of my teammates to share in the most precious privilege—access to a radio. Our bonds deepened through these interactions and conversations in the instructors' office. And so, by being the *House Mouse*, I had the opportunity to strengthen my partnership with each member of my flight. It was as

I recalled the one place where we were relaxed and enjoyed the usual conversations about all different kinds of topics.

After several weeks of intense training, my unit was selected to be the honor flight within the entire training squadron. The selection was based on aggregate academic record, physical fitness achievements, and the least demerits (violations or infractions during the training). With additional practice sessions to sharpen our drilling skills, my flight trained at every opportunity to synchronize our marching abilities for graduation. We were told beforehand that our flight would have the honor to march in front of all the other flights in our squadron, and thus, we had to be the best. On graduation day, along with several hundred airmen from the other training squadrons, my flight marched as the lead. I was selected to salute the officer who was officiating the graduation ceremony. As I led my team marching, all of us pushed hard on our left and right heels in unison on the concrete pad. I approached the senior officer on the reviewing stand, with my team behind me. I pulled up my right hand, placed it into position a few inches from belt buckle, turned my head to the right, continued marching with my team, pulled my hand to my face with my index finger barely touching my right eyebrow, and saluted. With the salute still in place, I led my team behind me and followed my unit's blue honor flag in front of me, away from the reviewing stand. It was a wonderful feeling, as we, as a group, had graduated! Basic training was finished! And now we were airmen of the US Air Force, and each anxiously waiting for our first duty assignment was ready to leave the dormitory forever.

Graduation from basic training was a significant achievement for me. For, my teammates too. For all of us, it was a relief and an opportunity to look forward to our job assignment. From my team members' first marching event on the night we all met for the first time to the graduation ceremony, it was an incredible transformation, from civilians with long hair into crew-cut professional airmen. The transformation showed how two training instructors (leaders) managed to change the attitudes and posture of forty young men into airmen ready for duty. The training curriculum, athletics, and field exercises were managed in such a way to turn a group of individuals into a cohesive unit that was ready to begin duty anywhere in the world. Each member shook the hand of each instructor and thanked them for all their help, mentorship, and perseverance during basic training. It was a fond farewell. I never ever saw them or heard from them again. However, I always remembered their names and what they accomplished as noncommissioned officers to transform civilians into airmen, including myself, and to transform us to be ready for duty. It was indeed an incredible transformation of ordinary young men into members of the US Air Force.

Almost all of my classmates were sent on to technical schools for on-the-job training. A few, including me, went on to direct duty assignments. I was assigned to Kelly Air Force Base, which is about a couple of miles from Lackland Air Force Base. And so, after graduation, my intense regimented life ended, and I began my career in the US Air Force as an airman.

After checking with my new unit (Communication Squadron) at Kelly Air Force Base and completing the in-processing, which took a couple of days, I went home to visit my family in New York City. The meeting was joyous; I was delighted to see my parents and sisters and eat my mother's food again, without having to stand in line. After an hour or so at home, I felt different and changed, in a sense of being more responsible and more confident, and just waiting to see the world. It was a feeling of accomplishing a monumental achievement (transforming from a civilian into an airman), which was still slowly becoming embedded in my thoughts, and a belief that other challenges could be accomplished through determination, perseverance, and hard work. Basic training transformed me into an airman and provided the foundation to further build a career in the air force and in my personal life in general.

Reflections on Substantive Assignments

My first assignment—communications specialist. As a new airman in the communications center at Kelly Air Force Base in San Antonio, Texas, I had obviously had the lowest rank. I had one brand new stripe and was very proud of it. The communications center was essentially the hub for all incoming and outgoing written communication to key officials throughout all air force bases and, thus, critical for the base commander's mission. It was a place that operated 24 hours a day and 365 days a year. It was indeed a place of much activity as I came to learn very soon on my first day at the center. Those were the days of teletype and, at that time, high tech.

Reporting to the communications center, the highest-ranking noncommissioned officer (NCO), a master sergeant, greeted me with friendly eye contact and enthusiasm that I still remember. Still fresh from my basic training experiences and very respectful of everyone who had a rank higher than me, I stood at attention when he spoke to me. As he spoke, I listened. I said little and just followed him. He escorted me into the various work sections and introduced me to his team. Each welcomed me and offered words of encouragement. The master sergeant's warm welcome, as I recalled, was meant to reassure me that basic training was over and I should relax when around senior airmen. I took his word. I believed in him and trusted him. But sometimes, however, I was still edgy around him, considering my basic training experiences were etched in my mind. Indeed, he appeared to be particularly humble, calm, and courteous.

I thought it was not normal for one with such a professional demeanor. Basic training was over, and I was now in the real Air Force. He also seemed to be very sincere and appeared to be well-liked and respected. I came to learn later he was a very devoted family man and deeply religious. Coming from the Midwest, he projected a relaxed and quiet professional demeanor, and he never lost eye contact when speaking to me and to others, as I observed him. From my first meeting with him, I admired him and was impressed with the way he projected himself. Him being very organized, considering the responsibilities he had, I immediately had high respect for him—always did. As I came to know him later, he was particularly a very good person, a trusted mentor, and a leader, and he never seemed to lose his self-control and his confidence. As a leader, he was well-known for his memorandums to all personnel two to three times a week, which were posted on the center's official bulletin board. His points were informative and well-read by everyone in the center. For me, it was the first thing I would read after I entered the center each day of duty, and I looked forward to each opportunity.

Considering the importance of the communications center, there were essentially three teams—each working eight hours, to ensure maximum coverage through a twenty-four-hour cycle. At the end of the month, a team was assigned the next shift. And so during my assignment in the communications center, I changed shift each month and reported to the same civilian supervisor (an air force veteran), with a noncommissioned officer (NCO), a staff sergeant as his deputy.

Without having to go to technical school to learn about my new job, I was designated to have on-the-job training. This proved to be a good concept as it allowed some airmen to report to duty and learn the job without in-residence training. It was, however, very demanding. Under the scrutiny of the master sergeant, who planned my training program, I was also mentored by my civilian supervisor and his staff. The training was very organized. These were dedicated professionals with years of experience. This helped me to establish the basic foundational knowledge and then build on that. With periodic tests, my supervisor certified that I was learning the required elements for the job.

I was always under the watchful eye of my civilian and military supervisors. Within set time limits, I soon began to operate independently and take on more complex tasks, and with that came more self-confidence. As a member of the team, I could not have begun to do my work independently without the help of my supervisors and teammates. Their help was instrumental for me to understand complex processes, with varying degrees of supervisory quality controls. In addition, without the help of my senior NCOs, it would have been difficult to become so quickly proficient in my job. The NCOs were instrumental, and their leadership (their approach to do and get their assignments done) served to keep the communications center's operations running as smoothly as possible. Not only were they professionals in their air force work, but also they were very caring for single and lower-ranking personnel, always taking a genuine interest to get everyone in the workplace (including civilians) involved in social and sports activities to keep our self-confidence high. It resulted in further bonding the camaraderie among each other.

At the start of my assignment, the emphasis on improving one's education was a persistent theme. My team's senior NCOs encouraged everyone to use their spare time effectively by taking advantage of the air force educational opportunities and from the colleges and universities in San Antonio. Following their advice, I did not want to waste my time. My goal was to learn as much as possible to make usage of every educational opportunity. Following the encouragement and support of my civilian and NCO supervisors, I enrolled to take college courses from one of the local colleges in San Antonio. With shift work, my supervisors accommodated me. Without any special privileges, they split my "weekend" so that I could have Tuesdays and Thursdays off in order to take college courses. Though working shift work and taking college courses were a little problematic, it was nevertheless only possible with my supervisors' support. Going to college not only broadened my academic skills but also gave me an opportunity to interact with civilians in my age group in San Antonio and learn more about the city and its culture. Taking college courses and serving in the air force was a rewarding experience as it benefited not only me but also the US Air Force.

About eight months or so, I was assigned more responsibilities. Meeting all my training requirements and having passed my examinations, I was promoted within the expected time. With added responsibilities, my military career began to take shape. Besides my military superiors, I was also mentored by other dedicated air force civilians. I was very fortunate to have my civilian supervisor taking a special interest in me, with encouraging words to continue to get my college degree. His help and advice gave me the self-confidence to do work within strict quality standards and also to increase my confidence in what I was required to do.

At about my two-year point in active duty, I decided it was time for me to return to college full-time. I pursued opportunities in the active Air Force Reserve through the Palace Chase program. This program allows an active-duty airman to leave active duty and participate in the active reserve. The requirement was that one had to serve two months in the reserve for each month of active duty time remaining. The reserve commitment was one weekend a month and two weeks each year.

As my active duty came to an end, I began to realize the importance of the work I did and what I learned in the communications center. With my colleagues and me, we were one link of a network to support key officials at the base so that they could accomplish their mission. It was an important mission that facilitated the flow of critical information throughout the base to worldwide customers. But soon, as I increased my proficiency, I began to notice that more responsibilities were given to me. The slow but certain transformation of me had begun to take place—the air force, with its training programs and structure, had given me the opportunity to perform work that was of major importance. The trust and my senior commissioned and noncommissioned officers (NCOs) with whom I worked made the transformation process easy.

During my last few days, as I began to prepare for my departure, I felt a sense of satisfaction of accomplishment in what I did in the communications center at Kelly Air Force Base. Assigned to rotating teams, which changed every month, I felt that in some way, I contributed to the air force mission. Through this job, I learned more and more about the US Air Force and its mission. It is an exceptional organization, with members from every corner of the United States and every ethnic background, doing important things to maintain freedom. From my vantage point in the communications center, I worked with some of those airmen.

The last few days were memorable as my teammates and closest friends began to organize social activities in my honor. With coworkers from California, Louisiana, Massachusetts, Michigan, Montana, South Carolina, New York, and Texas, we used our free time for fun activities. With trips to the Texas/Mexico border, Houston, the hill country nearby Austin, exploring San Antonio, and New Braunfels and the picnicking along the Guadalupe River, it was an exciting time. Driving through many back roads, enjoying Mexican food, drinking Lone Star beer, and shooting pool during several barhopping trips during the weekends, my air force friends did things for fun but always within self-control not to get in trouble with the police and lose our security credentials. From saying farewell on my last long night to special friends on the base, I departed Kelly Air Force Base for New York City. Leaving as a new member of the United States Air Force Reserve, I took with me a new outlook on life and experiences that shaped my life in the years ahead.

My commission and then an intelligence officer/planner. Early on in my reserve career, my commander, other officers, and NCO colleagues encouraged me to get a commission after I earned my college degree. After years of part-time college attendance and supplementing my income with numerous part-time jobs, I completed my college degree. With a college degree in hand, I immediately began the process to get a commission. The process, though detailed, required testing, a nomination from my reserve commander, and letters of recommendation. After putting together a detailed package—letters of recommendation from numerous individuals from my community, including my congressman—I competed with others in the reserve for a commission. I learned the good news from my commander (whose civilian job was a practicing lawyer in New York City) when he called me while I was on an assignment in Stuttgart, Germany. After attaining the rank of technical sergeant, I received my commission in 1987 and pinned on my brand new second lieutenant gold bars at McGuire Air Base, New Jersey, in front of all my colleagues.

After commissioning, I was offered the opportunity to select a career field. I selected human intelligence based on the advice offered by several officers and an NCO in my unit. My decision to select human intelligence was because of the opportunities to travel overseas and work with colleagues from the different branches in the military and with other federal agencies. With the commission and the new career field, additional worldwide opportunities became a reality.

Not long after I received my commission, I attended an officer orientation course at Lackland Air Base Annex—returning to Lackland for training this time was more straightforward as compared to my enlisted basic training. With my enlisted background, I thought the material will be easy, and it was. Other colleagues in the orientation course also had some military background, and for the most part, the orientation course was just that, an orientation course. The training focused on a number of topics, including air force history, the air force organization, and leadership. With the lectures, the themes meshed together to stress how the air force expects its officers to be effective while on duty and off duty. My classmates were all intellectually and physically focused on the training, and as a team, we earned and graduated with the honor class designation.

At graduation, Mr. Lee Greenwood's song "I Am Proud To Be an American" was played prior to the start of the ceremony. The song was played as the first item on the graduation agenda, and it stirred everyone into a patriotic spirit. It was indeed the most appropriate patriotic song for airmen to hear as we were about to be sworn in as air force officers. After the national anthem and the graduation ceremony, the guest speaker, an air force brigadier general, implored all the new officers to serve the nation and the air force with distinction. The graduation ceremony ended with everyone singing the Air Force Song[11] with an enthusiasm I had ever heard yet.

With a commission and the completion of the Air Force Officer Orientation Course, I was placed in a position with more responsibilities, as an intelligence officer. But with my enlisted training and as a former NCO, I had a deep appreciation for my new role and responsibilities as an officer. As a human intelligence officer, the challenges ahead were monumental, and the opportunities immense.

With a robust training program in the United States and overseas, I slowly began to increase my operational skills in the intelligence arena. Training included topics of international affairs and

---

[11] The Air Force Song

> Off we go into the wild blue yonder,
> Climbing high into the sun;
> Here they come zooming to meet our thunder,
> At 'em boys, Give 'er the gun! (Give 'er the gun now!)
> Down we dive, spouting our flame from under,
> Off with one helluva roar!
> We live in fame or go down in flame. Hey!
> Nothing'll stop the US Air Force!

political issues. These I found to be very informative and beneficial. Some training included interrogation field exercises to cope with prisoners in a wartime situation and how to interrogate within legal international parameters. The training was led by very experienced air force personnel, and as a new one in this career field, I had much to learn from the experts. These training exercises simulated tactical situations, and to build on leadership skills, each student had alternating roles. I had the opportunity to learn under the tutelage of some experienced experts to manage some aspects of a tactical exercise. The experiences I gained from such exercises continue to sharpen my skills, my confidence, and my overall abilities as an officer.

As an intelligence officer, I began to understand how I fit in the air force's mission to the defense of the nation. Using information, I soon began to author reports. Assessments gave me the opportunities to think deeply about international issues, the facts, and draw objective conclusions. An assessment is perhaps the most important function of the intelligence officer. It allows the officer to think about the facts and write objective summaries, without any personal bias for decision-makers.

Going from one assignment to another and interacting with individuals from many organizations, I learned more about the importance of what I did. It was during various military exercises in Germany, Greece, Korea, and Turkey that I began to see how intelligence products help elected leaders craft policy. Through some military exercises, I saw how commanders using intelligence to craft policy. They relied on intelligence officers to help them to achieve their mission objectives. As a result, my role as an intelligence officer began to be clearer in my mind and, more importantly, what was expected of me.

In 1998, as an employee of the University of North Florida, Jacksonville, Florida, I had the opportunity to meet a high-ranking civilian[12] who visited the university to speak about NATO expansion

---

[12] Senior executive service

and the NATO's Partnership for Peace program.[13] The gentleman, who was the deputy defense advisor to the United States Mission to NATO, in Brussels, Belgium, was traveling around colleges and universities' campuses in the United States speaking on what NATO was doing to invite former Soviet republics to join NATO. As he ended his campus visit, he invited me to do my reserve duty in his office in Brussels that summer, upon learning that I was an air force Reservist.

My commander gave me permission to do my reserve duty at the defense advisor's office in the US Mission Office to NATO during the summer of 1998. Flying into Brussels, Belgium, and checking in with the defense advisor the next day in the US Mission to NATO was exciting for me. The US Mission to NATO is led by an ambassador, the US primary officer to NATO, and within the mission is the Office of Defense Advisor. The defense advisor is the highest-ranking Department of Defense employee and who advised the US ambassador to NATO.

The defense advisor's responsibilities are immense and complex. The office had about four officers (colonels and lieutenant colonels) and a few civilians. As a major, I was the youngest officer associated with the defense advisor's office. Yet despite my rank, I was invited to as many of the North Atlantic Council's[14] meetings to accompany the defense advisor's deputy. My access to the council's meetings gave me an incredible opportunity to listen and see how US and NATO policies were made, through consensus. To see this dynamic in which NATO's national representatives discuss issues of vital importance to NATO and to their respective countries was very helpful to understand what was important to the United States. My role, however, was more than listening—it was to take notes and write summary cables for the defense advisor to be forwarded to the Office of the Secretary of Defense. This responsibility was demanding most of the time. An average duty day was about ten to twelve hours, with numerous interactions with colleagues in the United States, where

---

[13] Partnership for Peace Program: A NATO organization with members of the former Soviet Union to collaborate and work on issues of mutual interest.

[14] NATO's highest policy making body—essentially, national ambassadors, chaired by the Secretary General of the organization.

the time difference between Belgium and the United States required one at the US Mission at NATO to work a longer day.

The issues discussed in the North Atlantic Council were essential to gain consensus. Consensus is perhaps the most important concept within NATO, relating to policy decisions. As such, decisions are made only after every national representative agrees with a proposed policy after all nations have had the opportunity to discuss and offer modifications to change a policy. During my visit, the top issue for discussion was the political situation resulting from the breaking up of Yugoslavia. The discussions were lengthy and time-consuming. But considering the issues and the implications for security in Europe, it had to be extensive in that all nations were concerned that this was a crisis that could have major implications for NATO's and Europe's security. This issue arose because it appeared that Russia had indicated publicly it will have a say to protect Serbia's national interest, its ally based on historical cultural links and some common political ideology.

This duty was a first for me in the world of policy making in an international diplomatic setting. It gave me a unique opportunity to work with an incredible group of military officers (air force, army, marine, and navy), Department of Defense civilians, and political officers from the Department of State to craft reports for policy makers in the United States who had responsibilities for managing US policy toward NATO. Working with US diplomats and interacting with those from NATO's member nations gave me a deeper appreciation of the role of the US military and the importance of the civilian control of our nation's military. Compared with my other assignments, it was the first time where I saw firsthand from the US Delegation the importance of comportment. Members of the US Delegation sitting behind the US ambassador or designee in the NATO's conference room are noticed in that for the most part, all seats designated to the United States are taken. The US Delegation always with a full contingent shows to member nations that the United States takes its role very seriously. Other nations do as well, but for the most part, their delegation is much smaller than the United States.

It was clear from my first day attending meetings in the North Atlantic Council that all my background knowledge on international relations and writing and oral skills were needed and were vital to understand and contribute to the US Delegation's mission. My responsibilities in this assignment were not a traditional air force job, but one that required frequent interaction with individuals with the Department of State and the Department of Defense (Office of the Secretary of the Defense and the Joint Chiefs of Staff), and this broadened my perspectives as to the role of military officers in the civil military relationship and the civilian control of the US military.

Discussions about the deterioration of events in Bosnia-Herzegovina were detailed and substantive. The diplomats' choice of words showed the importance for precise language to communicate ideas and thoughts. It became more evident when agreements were documented into policy statements—the importance of words became more critical to ensure the meaning was clear for consensus among member nations. When more clarity was required, the British ambassador would occasionally and in all seriousness and sometimes with humor request minor changes such as "and," "the," or a "comma" to a policy document for clarity. The little changes are important and most times helped to get consensus with partner nations.

My two weeks with the defense advisor was enlightening and very rewarding. In the end, I came to realize that air force officers were doing work beyond the traditional air force mission. The fact that air force officers were integrated with other members in other branches of the uniformed services showed that military personnel were partners to support their civilian counterparts in the Department of State on issues related to policy making. My assignment with the defense advisor opened my mind to new ideas and new perspectives on my role in the Air Force Reserve.

Had not the defense advisor invited me to work with him, I would never have had such a fabulous opportunity to see firsthand how US policy relating to NATO was shaped. His offering me the opportunity was indeed a lucky break. Later, on my last day, he told me he was a retired US navy captain, and he understood the importance of assisting lower-ranking personnel. He reached out to me, and for that, my experiences in the summer of 1998 created new perspectives for me and my future Air Force Reserve career. As we said goodbye, he offered me another invitation for the following year, and I immediately accepted. He told me because I understood the issues and had a keen understanding of the US positions, he wanted me to return to work with his team.

I returned to Brussels in the summer of 1999. The major issue for discussion then at the North Atlantic Council was still the situation in the former Republic of Yugoslavia. The situation in Bosnia-Herzegovina and Kosovo was beginning to become more volatile. Partner nations within NATO were beginning to debate the situation more vigorously. The US ambassador and delegated representatives made the US case and with other nations tried to reach a consensus on what NATO should do. My role was to continue to support the defense advisor and his team. As before, I attended meetings in the North Atlantic Council with the US Delegation, took notes, and wrote summary cables. The cables synthesized the meetings and requested guidance from the Joint Chiefs of Staff or the Office of the Secretary of Defense. The requesting of guidance was a key tool for the US team in that guidance from our superiors gave the US Delegation the authority to clarify or discuss US positions in meetings. This control gave policy makers in Washington more oversight in negotiations.

My two weeks duty in 1999 was to some degree similar to the previous year. The processes were the same, but the issues were more complex. The US Delegation (US diplomats and the defense advisor) always try to understand other nations' positions and facilitate the process so that NATO could reach a consensus. The opportunity to see the senior leaders discuss and brainstorm issues gave me a rare opportunity to learn about US policy making. The dynamics of policy making were new to me, and the opportunities of 1998 and 1999 offered a unique insight to see how senior leaders interact to achieve US objectives in an international forum.

Within weeks after I returned home after my NATO assignment, I was offered a permanent Air Force Reserve position with the US Military Delegation to NATO's Military Committee as an intelligence officer to support the US military representative (a three-star general officer), whom the defense advisor recommended me for. The officer (lieutenant colonel) in the position had received a promotion, and he was transferred to another position. With my experiences with the defense advisor's office, I was a good fit. The lieutenant general (US Army) reviewed my package and approved it making it possible for me to join his team, US Military Delegation to NATO's Military Committee.

In April 2000, I reported to the US Military Delegation to NATO's Military Committee. This organization, led by the lieutenant general (US military representative), who represents the chairman of the Joint Chiefs of Staff to NATO. The US military representative had a support staff of about six colonels and a one-star deputy general officer. Other support staff included a few lieutenant colonels, US navy commanders, and NCOs. My responsibilities entailed oversight of all intelligence policy issues within NATO. With this position, I was again able to use my background knowledge on international relations, my experiences as an intelligence officer, and my familiarity with how NATO works while I worked for the defense advisor at the US Mission to NATO during the summers of 1998 and 1999. As a major (the lowest ranking officer/planner in the delegation), this was truly a hard-to-believe assignment. To interact with high-ranking visitors from the United States gave me a unique opportunity to represent the US Air Force Reserve and learn from some brilliant officers from each of the different branches of the uniformed services.

From 2000 to 2009, I had opportunities to directly interact with four US military representatives to NATO, one from each branch of service (army, air force, marine, and navy). As an airman, this was indeed my top assignment since being in the Air Force Reserve. The Military Representative Office had an important mission, and it dealt with a very broad portfolio of issues involving US interests at NATO and with the Partnership for Peace organization.

I participated in six of NATO's Crisis Management Exercises, designed and structured to have all NATO members participate in a scenario to test each alliance's member's abilities to respond to crises that could impact every ally in the alliance. Moreover, the exercises were designed to be as realistic as possible in order for NATO policy makers to understand the challenges and issues that they could face in a real contingency. It was indeed in the exercises and through deliberations that NATO's member nations make decisions that could set precedence or give an insight as to how a nation would react in a real emergency. During each exercise, my other reserve colleagues (different service branches) arranged and managed a coordination center to analyze all incoming pieces of information and provide inputs to the US military representative and his team on substantive issues relating to the US positions. As with most military exercises, these at NATO provided the opportunities to interact with the US ambassador and his political officers and with individuals at the Joint Staff in the Pentagon. These interactions broadened my perspectives into policy making, the US national decision-making processes, and the military's role in providing input for political leaders to make decisions of national importance.

The NATO exercises also afforded me opportunities to meet officers from countries within the NATO alliance. As a member of the Reserve, the opportunities to interact with officers from NATO were invaluable. Speaking to the officers gave me insight into their personal perspectives and their countries' strategic interests and, more importantly, their country's stance on issues relating to the alliance. I have found that in discussions with officers on a one-on-one basis, I learned more. An international officer's personal perspectives gave me a deeper insight into looking at international issues from a different angle. And through the discussions, I began to understand the importance of other individuals' perspectives at a multilateral organization. Moreover, it gave me the opportunity to explain my views on my country's position on international issues. There were disagreements, but they make you think. Overall, the opportunities to engage with international officers were priceless.

A deployment to support the war on terror—country director (Pakistan) at Headquarters, Central Command, MacDill Air Force Base, Tampa, Florida. In August 2005, I was promoted to the rank of lieutenant colonel in a unit vacancy. Essentially, I competed for a promotion, one year earlier than the required time-in-grade requirement. Based on my earlier accomplishments and potential to work at the next grade level, the promotion board approved my promotion to lieutenant colonel.

After receiving the promotion, several of my colleagues and mentors advised me to compete for a slot at the Air War College. While I had never thought of attending the college, a letter from the Air Reserve commander congratulating me on my promotion and encouraging me to apply gave me the impetus to follow through. The commander's letter also reinforced the importance of air force training and its importance to growing within the organization. I felt that not applying would go against the advice of my commander. Similarly, I would lose a coveted opportunity to broaden my educational experiences.

I submitted my application to the Air Reserve Selection Board to compete for a slot. The process was highly competitive as it is to be expected for those who have attained the rank of lieutenant colonel. The selection board reviewed each application, and if someone were selected, he or she was then placed in one of the several slots in each of the senior military schools (Air War College, Army War College, Navy War College, and National Defense University). A few months later, I learned I was one of seven reservists (Air Force Reserve's allocation to the class of 2008) that got selected to attend the Air War College, the air force's premier professional educational institution for lieutenant colonels and colonels. I was enthusiastic about the news, and my Air Force Reserve colleagues congratulated me on my selection. My civilian employer at the time, the University of North Florida, in Jacksonville, Florida, had always been very supportive of my Air Force Reserve commitment during the eleven years I have been associated with the institution. And in accordance with the federal rules and regulations pertaining to reservists, the university granted me a leave of absence to attend the Air War College in-residence program, starting in June 2007, in Montgomery, Alabama.

My Air War College experience had the greatest impact on my educational experiences (more on this in the next section). Halfway through my program, I decided to do more active duty. I wanted to put to use what I learned and what I was learning. I could not wait to do so.

I explored job opportunities with active duty and with the Reserve and got an offer as the country director for Pakistan at Central Command Headquarters, MacDill Air Force Base, in Tampa, Florida. The position was within the J-5 (Directorate for Strategy, Policy, and Plans). When the offer was made to me, I advised the branch supervisor that I could not speak Urdu, but I had some background knowledge on political issues in Afghanistan, Pakistan, and India. He said the language would be useful, but it was not required for the job. He also said he was confident I could do the job based on my education and work experiences. He advised me to read everything I could get my hands on about Pakistan, Afghanistan, and India. I took his advice and spent much of my free time in the Air War College library, going through books and magazines on the three countries.

I reported to the supervisor for the Central Asia and South Asia Branch on June 23, 2008, to begin work. Excited I could put to use what I learned in the Air War College, my first day as the country director exposed me to many of the things I learned in the Air War College, such as national interests, terrorism, regional security, US national decision-making processes, congressional funding, the United Nations, nongovernmental organizations. Within a week, I realized that almost everything Central Command did with respect to security cooperation in Pakistan passed through my desk. As the focal point for these issues relating to Pakistan, I felt I had more responsibilities than I ever had before. I knew that more will be expected of me, and I was ready for the challenge. I was also happy and honored to be contributing to the war on terror and always thinking on what new ideas to defeat those who wanted to destroy the United States of America.

As the country director, I was the primary point to receive, analyze, and provide information relating to security cooperation programs between the United States and Pakistan. Security cooperation programs are essentially a package of steps by which the United States can strengthen its partnership with foreign countries. In my job, I was charged with ensuring that the US partnership with Pakistan was strengthened.

The intensity of the job was mind-blowing—it was ten to twelve hours a day, with most of the time a few minutes for lunch. On the weekends, in order to stay abreast on fast-flowing issues, I would work, for the most part, at least half a day or a whole day. Also, on most weekends, the deputy J5, a one-star navy admiral, would work. Most times, we were the only ones in the directorate and working together on common issues. As a brilliant officer, with incredible human relations skills, he later got promoted to vice admiral.

Information constantly poured in from the US Embassy in Pakistan, the Department of State, the Department of Defense, the Office of the Secretary of Defense, the Joint Chiefs of Staff, component commands, and almost every key office within Central Command (CENTCOM). It was my responsibility to manage the information flow, with inputs from my colleagues, to ensure the commander of Central Command and his key officers had the most up-to-date information on Pakistan. My discretion to determine what was important and how much information to send up the chain became obvious as my knowledge increased. My portfolio sometimes had about eight or nine key issues, and each had key individuals in various US agencies with some oversight. It was my responsibility to coordinate with these individuals to inform them of CENTCOM's positions and determine what other steps needed to be taken to achieve the goals the commander of CENTCOM had established. It was through my interacting with the commander and his key officers that I came to know and understand what was important to them, how they managed their time, and what they needed to make decisions.

Using this understanding, I did the coordination—determined the status of key items for the commander and other senior leaders. Despite the long work hours, I enjoyed the work and felt this was a time to really contribute to the war on terror. Each morning, I went to work with a positive attitude to support the commander of CENTCOM and my colleagues and do what was necessary with regard to strengthening the relations between the United States and

Pakistan. I knew the work was important and felt that a positive attitude was the only way to get the work done.

With Pakistan being a key US partner in the war, I was convinced the position as the country director would open opportunities for me to make substantive contributions. Every day, it seemed that issues relating to security cooperation matters increased and became more complex as the need to strengthen the partnership between the United States and Pakistan was ever more pressing. My branch supervisor[15] told me it would take about six months to become proficient on all the issues, and he was right. Each issue had a set of complex policy concerns to learn and understand. For example, in the business of security cooperation, there were financial matters, military capabilities, military equipment and functions, strategy, policy, national and domestic politics, and regional security issues to contend with. In the case of Pakistan, there were broad political, financial, and strategic matters to consider. Understanding each US agency's position was key to develop information papers for Gen. David Petraeus and his staff to make decisions that impacted the partnership between the United States and Pakistan.

The most fulfilling aspect of this position was to accompany the commander when he visited Pakistan. During my assignment, I visited Pakistan five times and made one trip to India. These trips required a significant amount of preparation of trip books (information packages on the issues to be discussed). As the country director, I was essentially in charge to recommend to a large extent the issues the commander should discuss with senior Pakistani military officers and civilian political leaders, and with this discretion, I recommended the themes to deepen the partnership. This aspect of the job to prepare information packages for the commanders was indeed the most rewarding. It gave me the opportunity to think about what

---

[15] An army lieutenant colonel. He and also an experienced Department of Air Force civilian were the most helpful in guiding me in the position. As the former country director for Pakistan, he had acquired vast knowledge on the issues, and despite his busy schedule, he was very gracious to help. Notwithstanding the fact we had the same rank, he was my first-line supervisor, a superb mentor, and a dedicated professional soldier.

was necessary for regional security in terms of Pakistan's role in the region. Through this process, I proposed issues for discussion and prepared the necessary packages for the commander to use in his meetings with Pakistani officials.

As my knowledge base on Pakistan increased, so did my responsibilities. My participation in various issues in the US/Pakistan strategic partnership increased, and I began to interact frequently with other military and civilian colleagues in Washington, DC, and in Islamabad, Pakistan. The scope of the work in these interactions was more complex, more time-sensitive, and more demanding because of Pakistan's importance for regional security.

My trips to Pakistan gave me the opportunity to see how a senior commander interacts with his foreign counterparts. In my role to support the commander and his key officers, I was exposed to various aspects of leadership, international political issues, and US strategy and policy to Pakistan.

On various trips to Pakistani installations, I was afforded the opportunity to interact with Pakistani officers. The meetings enabled me to learn about Pakistan—especially the problems and challenges the country was facing to eliminate terrorists from its tribal regions. In one trip by helicopter to the tribal region from Islamabad, I accompanied one of CENTCOM's commanders, and I saw firsthand the difficulty of the terrain and the challenges the Pakistani Army's Frontier Corps[16] were confronted with. Pakistan's tribal region is a very harsh environment with rolling hills, mountains, and numerous valleys interconnected with very few paved roads. From the air, the landscape is spectacular and peaceful. But it is obvious this area is perfect for terrorists and extremists groups to hide and conduct military operations in Pakistan or cross over the border into Afghanistan to carry out their acts with impunity.

As I became more adept at the policy issues, I interacted more with CENTCOM's senior leaders and key officials. Moreover, I also met and worked with the Pakistani contingent of liaison offi-

---

[16] Indigenous militia responsible for security in Pakistan's tribal agencies and the North-West Frontier Province.

cers at CENTCOM. These opportunities gave me greater insight into Pakistan's concerns and what was needed to strengthen the US/Pakistan partnership. The degree to which I was involved exposed me to more complex security cooperation issues with Pakistan and gave me more exposure to senior leaders. These opportunities were tremendously helpful to gain new perspectives into solving complex policy issues and what it took to be successful.

With my deployment coming to an end in July 2009, I left with the appreciation that I had served my nation in an area that was crucial to winning the war on terror. My work with other extraordinary officers and NCOs helped the commander of CENTCOM and his key officers to manage the critical partnership between the United States and Pakistan. It was an incredible experience to see how senior military leaders lead and manage complex issues in the constraints of time and resources and within the policy parameters established by elected officials.

Prior to my leaving, a very smart and enthusiastic air force major (who was selected for promotion to lieutenant colonel) with impeccable credentials (a graduate from the Navy Postgraduate Center in Monterrey, California) and with superb writing skills was assigned to the position and after a couple of months of side-by-side collaboration. I turned over the controls to him and other team members. I was confident; I was turning over the controls to a fully competent and dedicated airman to manage all things concerning Pakistan.

For a reservist working in an organization, one usually hears the comment, "I never knew you are a reservist." This comment was made to me several times by colleagues during my last week at CENTCOM. It was not necessarily a very profound statement, but one that is intended as a compliment. For me, it is one that I may take as a slight depending on who is making the comment or as a compliment, but under self-control, I always think of an appropriate response. The comment is made to imply my performance was not indicative of me as a reservist, but of an active-duty officer, who is generally more perceived to be motivated and more productive. On my last day, I was presented with an award in recognition for my performance, and the comment "I never knew you are a reservist" was made by a colleague. When I looked at him, he quickly said he was impressed by my performance on the job. In retrospect, my assignment at Central Command was by far the most dynamic and most rewarding job I have ever had in my association with the US Air Force.

The benefits of military duty. The US Air Force together with its reserve component is an incredible organization. To have the privilege to serve along with many dedicated and smart Americans with a deep commitment to what our nation stands for has been a remarkable opportunity for me. The air force organization's prestige and power do not necessarily emerge from the vast amount of sophisticated equipment it has at its disposal, but from its people. Airmen of the highest caliber operate the equipment and keep the watch in the homeland and in numerous locations throughout the world. Airmen from all walks of life, from every ethnic background, and as members of a team sustain a complex organization with a colossal mission, as it is—to be vigilant and ready to serve, anytime and anywhere in the world within a moment's notice in protecting the United States of America and its allies.

Military service to a country founded on democratic ideals is an honorable profession. To know that most people in the world are not free, service to a democratic country is even more important because of threats from unstable places from various parts of the world. Service and duty are dependent on strong philosophical beliefs of freedom and the will to defend freedom. It is that will, the personal resolve, and the beliefs that motivate individuals to join and serve. For me, it was that, the love of country and freedom to live with the least government interference in my life, and the opportunities for me and my family to do whatever we wish to do. So the choice to serve was easy. The air force organization needs individuals who believe in the American ideals and the democratic institutions that keep and hold the country together. As a volunteer, any personal disenchantment with the ideals would have required me to discontinue my service, but that situation never occurred.

With respect to the profession of service in the military being honorable, it is the expectation that service should not be based on altruistic reasons. In an affluent free society like the United States, the profession of military service is to contribute to the protection of freedom, and not with a surreptitious expectation to enrich one's personal income. While income and wealth do help to live a comfortable life, there is really no expectation that one will become wealthy with one's military service. And so, service for me and for most of those I interacted with has been selfless and in the belief in freedom.

The events of the terrorists' attacks on September 11, 2001, further strengthened my philosophical beliefs in service. Had I not been an airman at that time, the attacks would have motivated me to join. But being in the reserve, I felt it was my duty to continue to serve now more than ever. Immediately after the attacks, I sought to volunteer in any military operation, but I was not recalled. I knew I had to do more, and I did. For example, I did, however, serve beyond my expected monthly commitment to the Air Force Reserve by performing duty with three organizations, during a three-year period, an average of six days duty each month. My goal was to contribute in my way to help the air force do whatever is necessary to protect the homeland and eliminate terrorists' safe havens overseas even though I was enrolled in my doctoral program. My obligations to my doctoral program were reduced somewhat to allocate more time to the air force.

In my Air Force Reserve career, I met some very impressive and talented citizen airmen.[17] These were Americans from all walks of life and who came from many states in the United States and some who live overseas. Some of my citizen airmen, friends, and colleagues I served with were lawyers (some corporate and others with their own legal practice), medical doctors, dentists, agricultural research scientists, commercial bank vice presidents, teachers, postal workers, police officers, federal special agents, stockbrokers, and entrepreneurs—just the average hodgepodge of careers for a group of average patriotic Americans. To serve with such a variety of individuals gave me a greater insight into American society and what they think and believe about their military service. Serving with some of these

---

[17] Citizen airman—part-time civilians and part-time service to the Air Force.

individuals in various places of the world shows the degree of their motivation and the love for their country and the Air Force Reserve.

Duty overseas was always special. Not only was it a chance to see a different area of the world, but also it was an opportunity to represent the United States. For example, my assignments in Belgium and trips to Pakistan and in India gave me the honor to represent the Air Force Reserve in forums, where the spotlight was on the US Delegation for leadership, ideas, and commitment.

In sum, serving the US Air Force and the Air Force Reserve represented a momentous event in my life that provided opportunities not available to others in the private industry. The opportunities shaped my professional life and gave me access to be a witness to policy issues most airmen only read about. Further, service gave me a more profound insight into US values, what it stands for, and why freedom must be defended.

Reflections on professional military education

The air force's training program's aim is simple and straightforward. It is to keep all air force members ready for deployment and perform their jobs with the utmost level of competence. I found air force personnel took their training seriously, and it was rare to find one who did not.

My air force training gave me the background knowledge to accomplish my organization's mission. Training is a serious matter considering the time and resources air force leaders allocate for such activities. Without these programs, the air force would not have the necessary qualified people to do its mission. More and more, it was reinforced that training is everyone's responsibility, and each had to make sure their respective training was completed. Furthermore, everyone must continue to train to do all their tasks so that all those airmen (e.g., pilots and policy makers) who depended on them can have the assurance that the most proficient and highly trained air force personnel are at the controls. It was that assurance that gave me confidence in air force systems and processes, and, more importantly, the competence of airmen.

Considering the scope of training that an average airman must take, the response to one's mission will come naturally while working in any environment with other highly skilled and dedicated airmen. The US Air Force and Reserve spent an incredible amount of money to educate me to get me ready and keep me ready for worldwide deployments at a moment's notice. Discounting my first master's degree, which was 100 percent funded by the G. I. Bill, I also had the privilege and honor to attend several in-residence courses and take some mandatory correspondence air force-sponsored courses.[18] I will comment on the most substantive courses and what I learned. The learning process was more than the actual instruction. It was also learning from fellow airmen speaking about their experiences as well, during class discussions.

The air force must have trained personnel to perform its mission. Training is a continuous process, with the objective to make sure all personnel maintain the highest degree of proficiency to do their job. As an intelligence officer, my training has been more than intelligence-focused. The training prepared me to think critically about strategic issues on those matters that are important to the protection of the US national interests. Additionally, the training was purposeful in that I could perform my duty anywhere and anytime, with colleagues from the United States and allied nations.

---

[18] —Air Force Counter Insurgency Course (USAF Special Operations School)
—Defense Language Institute, Monterrey, CA: Refresher German Course
—Air Force Basic Interrogation Course (student)
—Air Force Field Interrogation Course (student)
—Air Force Field Interrogation Course (source)
—Dynamics of International Terrorism (USAF Special Operations School)
—Cross Cultural Communications Course (USAF Special Operations School)
—Marine Air Ground Reserve Interrogation of Prisoners of War Course
—Squadron Officer School, by correspondence
—Air Command and Staff College, by correspondence
—Reserve Officer Joint Military Operations Course, Naval War College (in-residence)
—Air War College, Maxwell AFB, Alabama (in-residence)

My interrogation[19] courses, for example, were the most critical courses to prepare me for my wartime mission. These courses taught by very experienced officers (representing the different branches but mostly from the air force) were truly first-class. The curriculum focused on doing and managing issues that were important for the air force mission. Under the supervision of the air force's brightest and experienced interrogators and all with combat experiences, the training enabled individuals like me to learn how to manage prisoners of war.

As I recalled, the overall theme then was always to show the utmost respect to prisoners in accordance with international law when interacting with them. That was an overarching rule to conduct each class. Besides the basic dynamics of interrogation and running a hypothetical prisoner of war camp, there were training blocks on international law and leadership and the expectation of all air force personnel handling prisoners. With senior air force members to guide and mentor me, I knew I got the best training that was available. Later, when I was selected to attend the Marine Air Ground Reserve Interrogation of Prisoners of War Course, this was a unique opportunity to work alongside combat-experienced US Marines and a first for me. Interacting with and working alongside the Marines gave me a rare insight and firsthand experiences with extremely dedicated and professional individuals. These interactions were important because I learned about the US Marines' organizational structure and culture, which came in very useful later in my career.

The mandatory correspondence courses were time-consuming, voluminous, but enriching. With volumes of material, studying various aspects of the air force history and accomplished leaders, the materials were intended to prepare each airman to learn specific things for the current rank. The training also gave me substantive grounding important and necessary for consideration for the next rank. Each course required a lot of concentration and determination

---

[19] These courses were taught within the strictest oversight controls possible to protect prisoners, using the direct questioning method only.

to complete, accompanied by a mandatory closed book examination, within a fixed time period to complete each course. It was in these correspondence courses that I began to learn more and more about some US pilots (such as the Tuskegee airmen, Jimmy Doolittle "Doolittle Raid," Paul Tibbets, and Robert Lewis) in the Second World War and, later, who accomplished unbelievable things to shape the air force as an organization as it is today.

The Air War College was indeed my best intellectual experience, even when compared to my civilian undergraduate, graduate, and doctoral studies. This program led me to learn how to critically think about issues, analyze the US national decision-making processes, and examine how military officers are supposed to lead. The reading assignments were incredibly diverse, which were intended to broaden all students' background knowledge of critical issues and historical events. The idea to learn about historical events was important because one can see how individuals made decisions under adversity and the outcome. Without an understanding of former air force leaders' challenges, new air force leaders would not have the grounding of how the air force as an organization developed its organizational and equipment systems to accomplish its mission.

Writing assignments, on the other hand, were intended to sharpen one's ability to think. The Air War College program had numerous projects, with the goal to improve each student's writing ability. Writing at the colonel's level is different from that of a second lieutenant. At a colonel's level, writing requires thinking to achieve simplicity. Achieving simpleness is complex, and it results in clarity; however, that is not easy. This requires critical thinking, about purpose, precision, knowledge of the audience, and intended impact. My Air War College program emphasized all this. After I finished the program, I was selected for a one-year deployment to Headquarters, US Central Command, in Tampa, Florida. In my first week, I was writing memos for the commander, his staff, planners in the Office of the Secretary of Defense, and several US ambassadors.

For the most part, the Air War College curriculum probed into various international issues, such as the reasons why wars are fought, the nation's interests, and the processes that US agencies use to make decisions. The lectures and reading assignments were helpful to understand how US agencies contribute to the national decision-making processes and how information moves up the chain to the president's closest national security advisors and to the president. Understanding each step helped me to see how individuals outside my chain of command were key to help implement policies that are of vital interest to the United States.

Learning from active leaders (individuals who are in visible positions of leadership) is perhaps the most effective way to learn about leadership. The Air War College distinguished guest lecture series was intent on having various military leaders speak to students. The invited guests shared their experiences and the challenges they faced in making decisions. Understanding how one faces some adversity and how the individual makes a decision instills new ideas on leadership and a greater appreciation for the challenges to make a decision. I believe I learned some unique aspects of leadership and success from each guest speaker who gave a presentation on their experiences.

Interacting with international officers was another positive aspect of my Air War College experience. The interactions gave me a unique opportunity to learn about the culture and political dynamics of a foreign country and how foreigners see and perceive the United States. On a one-to-one interaction, I learned more from the international officers when they shared opinions privately. However, when in a group, they tend to be more cautious when speaking about political and international issues. Further, when alone, however, it is different; sometimes international officers willingly are more critical of their own governments and say more positive things about the United States.

I am convinced that all my air force education experiences were first-class. In every program, I learned something to do my job better. Moreover, it also helped me to understand why the air force and the reserve are important to protect the United States and its overseas interests.

PART II

Introduction

In this section, I will discuss my reflections and observations on leadership. Leadership is a key topic that has been frequently mentioned by senior leaders (general officers, senior noncommissioned officers, and high-ranking civilians) and discussed throughout my career but more so during the past fifteen years of it. Early on in my career, there was little discussion about leadership, but now the issue is more in vogue and becomes more important every day as organizations seek to find efficiencies to operate effectively. Today, the application and study of leadership are absolutely crucial for the air force to meet current and future challenges.

Leadership is an important issue of discussion, deliberation, and application within military organizations. Senior military leaders want to ensure everyone within their organizations has some concept of what it is, its importance, and how to put into practice some ideas to benefit everyone. In fact, it also is included in practically all professional military education or training programs to expand concepts of leadership and its applications for managing organizations. Effective leadership is critical for the military because of the greater need to lead complex organizations with a diverse team, in charge of monumental responsibilities. To be effective today, military leaders must have background knowledge of a variety of issues (e.g., military, budgeting, logistics, US domestic and international politics, the functions of international organizations, religion, culture, diplomacy, and human relations).

On an average day, military leaders are confronted numerous times to make decisions on issues that impact national security, saving lives, and spending American taxpayers' money. And so, leaders with effective leadership skills have enormous responsibilities to guide an organization to success. Considering the oversight by Congress and the press, leaders are also faced with the demands to be responsible and act within the limits of the law. As such, the continuing demands are key reasons military leaders need to act in accordance with the law and do what is morally right. The scrutiny from the public is an accepted American institution and thus carries with it enormous implications for military leaders. The expectation is that Americans expect military leaders to do what is right. While this expectation should not be seen as an inconsequential matter, it is nevertheless part of the civil/military dynamic and control of the military by civilians since the founding of the nation.

On the other hand, ineffective leadership can have grave consequences in an organization. In such a situation, a leader making the wrong decision or being indecisive can put people's lives in danger and ruin their own careers. And so, the issue of leadership must be studied. Knowing more about leadership and the effective attributes associated with this construct will help further their application in organizational activities. It is thus increasingly critical that effective and ineffective leadership attributes need to be identified, analyzed, and implemented in training programs so that many individuals have some background knowledge of what they are and how they can be applied for one to be effective.

As one who studied leadership and did a substantive academic examination on it, I believe some aspects of doctoral research and findings[20] have some useful applications for the military. As such, I will use my earlier academic work and complement with my observa-

---

[20] Essentially, my research was on the implication of policy changes on higher education leaders and the internal challenges they face in implementing policy changes. My qualitative research showed that educational leaders must:
1. Have steadfast philosophical beliefs about the need to broaden access for those who have been historically discriminated against.
2. Be aware of the value of affirmative action and diversity for educational institutions.
3. Practice a participatory style of leadership.
4. Commit the value of using teams and implement the usage of teams.
5. Exercise prudent discretion in implementing policy.

tions from my air force assignments to deliberate on what leadership is and how it can be applied for one to be effective. Additional focus will be on its implication not only for members of our armed services but also for everyone who is interested in the art of leadership.

I believe that leadership is not a science, but rather a sociological activity with deep interconnections involving various senses and behavioral factors and awareness of those factors and the constant implementation of these factors. To quote from my previous research, which highlighted new perspectives of leadership and the demands of leadership, I found the literature showed:

The study of leadership is unfinished, and it will continue because there is more to be learned from others. It needs to be studied because there is irrefutable evidence that new ideas of leadership continue to emerge from active leaders. By studying leaders, we can learn new perspectives on how to lead.[21]

The US Air Force is a complex organization.[22] It requires individuals with a vast array of different skills and abilities (diplomatic, technical, sociological, and scientific, to name a few) to protect the United States' and allies' airspace. To manage vast resources (equipment, money, and people), leaders must have the abilities with knowledge bases that scan different functional and educational areas.

Source: *Access to Higher Education: Leadership Challenges in Florida and South Africa*. Lanham, MD: University Press of America, 2005, pp. 104–106.

[21] Marty Z. Khan, *Access to Higher Education: Leadership Challenges in Florida and South Africa* (Lanham, MD: University Press of America, 2005), p. 111.
For a short narrative from 100 top leaders on issues of leadership, see the following: Lynne J. McFarland, Larry E. Senn, and John R. Childress, *21st Century Leadership: Dialogues with 100 Top Leaders* (Los Angeles, CA: The Leadership Press, 1994).

[22] As of June 2020 (Source: *Air Force Magazine*, Journal of the Air Force Association, June 2020, pp. 43–64), key statistics in the United States Air Force for 2019 are as follows:
Total Air Force active duty: 332,101
Total civilian personnel: 168,942
Total Ready Reserve (Air Force Reserve): 204,900
Fiscal Year 2019 Air Force Budget: $174,807,000,000
Total active duty aircraft inventory: 5,387
Total intercontinental ballistic missiles: 400
Total satellites: 77

Leaders must be insightful, have the ability to think critically, anticipate problems, have the empathy to deal with individuals with different cultural backgrounds and needs, and not be afraid to make decisions.

Reflections on Leadership

This section will discuss key attributes for effective leadership. While there are numerous attributes for effective leadership, I have found there are some distinct ones that an individual interested in the art of leadership must pay special attention to be an effective leader. These are now discussed below:

1. Sincere and passionate philosophical beliefs about one's organization's mission and purpose. For one to be effective, one must have sincere and passionate philosophical beliefs about the mission and purpose of one's organization. An individual who has these beliefs must continuously show that he or she has them in order to project a positive image toward what must be accomplished. These beliefs must naturally effervesce through oral communication, body language, and enthusiasm.

Without strong philosophical belief in an organization's mission, it is highly unlikely that one can be effective in his or her organization. This belief is critical because it shapes how an individual will react to others in the organization. Additionally, the image the individual projects with respect to the mission of the organization or the assignments with which the individual is given must be positive.

One with strong philosophical beliefs will demonstrate to others an excitement of a "fire in the belly" approach and outlook and push hard to achieve the organization's mission and purpose. You can see or feel that in thoughtful policy discussions or in brainstorming sessions from anyone with the "fire in the belly" mindset. Individuals who have such strong beliefs generally are more positive about their responsibilities and sometimes contribute more substantive ideas to the discussions. Sometimes, these individuals tend to take the initiative to think deeply about issues that will impact their respective organizations and generally are the ones that offer suggestions on how to solve problems. Such initiatives to speak and share ideas are absolutely essential and represent the innermost characteristics of leadership attributes that make up who an individual is. The degree and extent to which an individual demonstrates his or her beliefs for the good of the organization is a signal of one with an enthusiastic mindset. Those without such eagerness will project a lack of interest to do anything. Such lack of interest is indicative of a negative malaise through distinct attitudes, such as tense facial features, minimal eye contact, and lack of focus.

When one is enthusiastic, one shows one's passion through a positive outlook. On the other hand, when one is unenthusiastic, it is common that such individuals generally do not depict themselves in a positive manner. As such, it reveals publicly a key attribute that they are uninterested and unwilling to contribute any substantive ideas for the good of the organization. An unenthusiastic outlook does much to project a negative attitude. It also reinforces an outward and noticeable impression of a general lack of interest when partaking in substantive and meaningful discussions.

One's beliefs for the most part guide an individual to set goals and the steps to achieve them. You can see this from written or oral communication from such an individual. In my work assignments at the United States Mission to the EU and NATO, US Military Representative's Delegation to NATO, and Headquarters, Central Command (CENTCOM), I have had on numerous occasions to be in the presence of general officers and high-ranking civilians discussing policy issues. The words they use, their enthusiasm for the issue, and their willingness to probe deeply into issues and problems that could affect the United States' national interests (the things that are important for the US vis-à-vis in its relations with other countries, allies, and alliances) show the passion with which these individuals have for the work they do. Moreover, during discussions, the questions they ask more often give useful clues as to what is important and not important to them and what it is they are trying to achieve.

For example, in the 1998–1999 time frame, I had the privilege to attend many meetings in the North Atlantic Council as a member of the US defense advisor's team with the United States Mission to

NATO. I recalled that during discussions of the crises in Bosnia and Kosovo (former Yugoslavia), the US ambassador had to articulate the US positions. The ambassador's words and especially his tone (to include delivery) were critical to showing how important this issue was for the United States. Likewise, other national ambassadors to NATO did the same. Without sincere belief in what one was doing, an ambassador could use words and tone that could misinterpret the message their nation wanted to articulate. In deliberations relating to Bosnia and Kosovo, the heightened concern for people (internally displaced persons) also showed how ambassadors were concerned for NATO's effectiveness in the crises and to what extent nations were willing to act to protect innocent civilians.

At the US Delegation to NATO, the US military representative (a three-star general officer)[23] represents the US positions at the Military Committee at NATO. During my duty assignments at NATO, I was invited to accompany the US delegation during NATO-related and Partnership for Peace[24] meetings. These meetings were of vital importance to the United States, in that they were used to strengthen the US relations for the benefit of European security. In all, the US military representative or sometimes his delegated representative articulated US positions with the goal to achieve consensus at the Military Committee at NATO. In those cases, when an issue is raised and the representative does not have the US position, he would likely say, "I have to consult with my superiors in my nation's capital for guidance." These words added credibility to NATO's policy making processes in that personal opinions rarely make policy; rather, it is from the guidance from one's representative capital in which the individual must articulate. Moreover, the deliberations highlighted the sincerity one must have to be effective at such a high-level meeting. The US representative, along with his colleagues, must deliver the right words to show the US and their respective nations' position,

---

[23] At this organization, I have had the extraordinary privilege and honor to serve directly to general officers (three stars) from the US Army, US Air Force, US Marines, and the US Navy.

[24] Partnership for Peace: A NATO organization that includes western and formerly Soviet Union countries. Russia, today, is part of the Partnership for Peace.

and not their personal opinion. To see the US military representative in action is to see how a leader represents his country in the world's premier military organization on issues that are vital to the United States' national and security interests.

At Central Command, I also had the privilege to attend many meetings with Gen. David Petraeus (US Army) and his deputy, Lt. Gen. John Allen (US Marines). In separate meetings with Gen. Petraeus in which he interacted with his general officers, he projected an image of immense sincere philosophical beliefs of what he had to do and what he wanted to achieve. His presence at meetings, the questions he asked, and his deliberation on issues illustrated one with tremendous sincere philosophical beliefs on what he has been charged to do. His words projected as one who understood the importance of what he had to do, and moreover, they established the tone with which his command must be led. Likewise, his deputy, Gen. Allen, also projected his beliefs of the importance of CENTCOM's mission through the usage of precise words to show the sincerity of what needs to be accomplished. Together, both of these general officers thoughtfully projected very strong beliefs about their organization's mission and what must be done to achieve US national objectives. For me, this was inspirational and learning experiences. It gave me some of the groundings for what I did in other air force assignments. Below are key steps to self-analyze one's leadership ability and how to focus on the mission.

Steps to develop strong philosophical beliefs about one's organization's mission and purpose:

1. Read the organization's mission—seek clarification from reporting officials and others in the chain of command on issues that are not clear. More specifically, determine:
   a. What it is the organization is tasked to do?
   b. What must be accomplished?
   c. Why it must be accomplished?
   d. What could happen within the organization if the mission is not accomplished?

    e.   What would be the impact on national security if the mission is not accomplished?
    f.   The reporting chain of command for your organization
        i.   Who are the key leaders?
        ii.   What are their leadership styles?
        iii.   Can you work for them? If not, what would one have to do to make sure there is a cordial relationship?
        iv.   Will you be able to get along with them (if in a direct reporting chain)?
2. Identify and read authoritative reference sources (e.g., documents from organizations within the chain of command or published articles) on the organization's mission and purpose:
    a.   Identify the purpose of the organization.
    b.   The historical legacy of the organization, if any, and what it has done for the common good?
    c.   Identify exceptional leaders in the organization and observe them in how they accomplish the organization's mission.
3. Do an introspective analysis of one's view of the organization's mission. More specifically, determine:
    a.   One's thinking about the organization's mission. Are there conflicts? If yes, determine what they are and what must be done to change one's negative feeling about the organization's mission.
    b.   Resolve professional conflicts with key officers in the reporting chain. Determine the root cause for each conflict and implement the steps and personal goals necessary to change the dynamics from a negative to a positive.
    c.   One's position and one's responsibility within the organization: If one is in a policy making position or has the responsibility for tasks that could impact lives, make sure there are no personal philosophical conflicts with the organization's mission.

d. Whether one can be effective in the organization if one does not agree with the organization's mission. If one does not agree with the organization's mission, determine what must be done to agree with the mission. Generally, it is unlikely for one to contribute positively to an organization if one does not agree with the organization's mission.
4. Strive to achieve a convergence of one's philosophical beliefs with one's organization's mission.
   a. Periodically make certain there are no conflicts. When there are, resolve them and make the appropriate compromises.
   b. Develop a continuous self-review to make sure that as the organization's mission changes, one's philosophical view of the organization does not conflict with the changes.
5. Determine the organization's senior leaders' philosophical perspectives on the organization's mission—ascertain this from what they say and do publicly and from their written communication to personnel within the organization.
   a. Does what they say conflict with the organization's mission?
      i. What they say and do publicly will impact how successfully they are in leading the organization.
6. Reflect on your knowledge of the organization and what the senior leaders are charged to do and refine your beliefs and thoughts to project strong philosophical beliefs of your organization's mission and purpose.

   2. Understand the president's national security strategy (NSS). Military personnel in positions of authority must understand what the president of the United States is trying to accomplish in their respective geographical area of responsibility. This knowledge is key to understanding one's mission and how one fits into their organization. Irrespective of one's duty, the NSS gives implicit information about one's role within an organization. For those individuals associated with an organization that has an overseas mission, the NSS is even more important to understand because it gives clarity on what the United States wants to achieve with its international partners.

The mission today for all military personnel is particularly very complex. I have met young airmen (perhaps three to five years in the service) during my overseas travel working in vital missions with broad responsibilities to protect the United States' interests. These young airmen along with others in higher ranks must understand the importance of their role to the mission and how it is linked to what the president wants to accomplish. Having such knowledge will help to strengthen one's value to his or her organization.

In all my assignments as an intelligence officer, I had the opportunity to read many reports pertaining to international relations and contribute to very important foreign policy issues my organization had within its mission domain. This coupled with my enthusiasm for international issues has broadened my mind and my background knowledge on what is important for the United States and what the president's foreign policy goals were. Having such background knowledge of the United States' interests helped me immensely to discuss issues, for example, relating to refugees in Darfur with European Union officials, the European Union's arms embargo against China, relations with NATO, Partnership of Peace countries, and Pakistan's role to support the United States in the war on terror.

At Central Command, I have seen that general officers articulated the need to strengthen partnerships within Asia. For me, the necessity to strengthen the partnership was obvious—the stronger the partnership, the more the United States can help to broaden democracy, help with humanitarian efforts, and also coordinate with US government agencies to help partner nations improve their free market economy.

Not having a grasp of national security issues limits one's value to an organization. And so, for one to be very effective to his or her military organization, broadening one's knowledge of the United States' national security strategy is absolutely critical. As such, every opportunity must be explored and pursued to achieve this.

Steps to enhance one's understanding of the mission and national security policy objectives:

1. Determine the president's national security policy objectives from primary sources, and ascertain:
   a. What does the president want to accomplish in a geographical area of responsibility?
   b. Why is it important for the United States?
   c. What is the impact if it is not achieved?
   d. What is your organization's area of responsibility and mission?
   e. What is your role in the organization?
      i. What is it that you must do to accomplish the President's National Security Strategy?
      ii. What background knowledge must one have?
2. Develop a keen understanding of the international issues (military, political, economic, and cultural aspects) pertaining to the president's national objective in your area of responsibility.
   a. Establish objective assessments to understand all aspects relating to the national security objectives.
3. Understand the importance of civilian control of the military.
   a. Any other belief than civilian control of the military would engender problems to implement the president's objectives.
   b. What are the organizational senior leaders communicating about the president's national security strategy?
      i. Positive statements are good.
      ii. Negative statements will impact the organization's path to achieve its mission.
4. Develop a personal reading program to read and be aware of the international issues relevant to the United States' interests.

3. *Follow a flexible combination of the participative and autocratic styles of leadership.* For any leader in the military, one's style or one's approach to leadership is crucial for success. From my observations, there is no particular leadership style for success; rather, I believe participatory and autocratic leadership styles appear to be most dominant, obviously with some degree of flexibility in the application of each. Nonetheless, both of these styles give a leader some flexibility to interact with subordinates and also motivate individuals to be productive members of a team.

By and large, I have found that a participatory style of management is applicable for most military situations; however, there are times when a leader must intercede at the most appropriate time (autocratic style) where there is ambivalence or reluctance to make a decision. When to intercede and the leeway to give colleagues or subordinates to lead require intuition, experience, and flexibility. However, knowing when is critical. If a leader procrastinates in making a decision, he or she could display apparent signs of an indecisive leader. In such a scenario, one could immediately lose all of one's credibility. Considering the complex issues military officers are responsible for, it is generally impossible for any individual to have absolute control over an organization's decision-making process—it would be overwhelming, creating distrust within the organization. Most importantly, it would stifle initiative and the diffusion of new ideas and create chaos and distrust.

Participatory leadership is essentially when a leader creates a cordial partnership environment for subordinates to offer input in the decision-making process, without the risk for censure from colleagues. Allowing others in an organization the opportunity to offer input for all intents and purposes is to empower an individual. This approach encourages individuals to take the initiative and learn about leadership. However, for this to be successful, senior leaders must delegate responsibilities to those who have the training, background knowledge, and motivation (positive philosophical beliefs on a mission) to take on such principal duties. Individuals cannot be fully functional or useful if they do not have the training, background knowledge, and positive philosophical beliefs on the mission of the organization. As a result, a leader must ensure all subordinates get the necessary training and sufficient resources to be effective in the organization.

The practice of participatory leadership, through time, engenders positive changes in climate within an organization. A positive climate serves as a safeguard against malaise or apathy, key factors that can impact an organization's achievement of its mission. Furthermore, a positive climate creates an environment where there is enthusiasm for participation in activities that are crucial for the organization's mission.

Individuals within organizations want and desire a sense of belonging; in essence, a need with some degree of status. In the military, despite the expectation of quality performance within the strict chain of command, personnel still have needs. Thus, it is through opportunities to participate in decision-making processes individuals can achieve their need for belonging to the organization. Even in the military where there is a culture for the expectation of quality performance and where selflessness is expected, individuals still have personal aspirations and are very conscious and sensitive about those factors that could affect their career ambitions. And when this happens, such individuals are not performing at their full potential.

Leaders have an enormous amount of discretion to fulfill their staff's desires and influence career expectations. With skillful instincts and perceptions, a leader may be able to galvanize the organization by soliciting others in the organization in the decision-making process. Being cognizant of the factors affecting individuals' motivation, a broad application of participatory leadership will ensure there are enthusiasm and an eagerness to accomplish the mission on time all the time.

Military organizations are generally known to practice an autocratic leadership style to control, with the belief that it guarantees absolute control of the system. Autocratic leadership generally connotes rigid guidance through inflexible directives—basically, only one person makes decisions, and there is generally no opportunity to offer advice or suggestions. For obvious reasons, there are situations where an autocratic style is needed, for example, in tactical situations whereby in order to execute a mission, the lives of individuals may be at stake. Sometimes, even in a tactical situation, alternative viewpoints can be very helpful. In other circumstances, where there is a lack of consensus to reach a decision because of differing views, the autocratic leadership style generally allows for a swifter process to make a decision. However, this is contingent on the leader's ability and background knowledge to make such decisions. With respect to effectiveness, an autocratic leader must have the ability to sense when is the right time to intervene and make a decision.

Reflecting on my experiences, I have encountered leaders who have practiced both the participatory and autocratic styles of leadership. I have seen how the participatory style of leadership allows individuals to share in the decision-making process and give them a voice in the process. To restrict others in the organization to have a say is to suppress the introduction of new ideas. Those individuals whose inputs are immediately rejected generally become uninterested in all matters pertaining to the success of the organization. A leader can strengthen his or her stature in the organization by encouraging and soliciting new ideas. The atmosphere in which individuals are encouraged to offer new ideas is important because it generates a feeling of belonging to a caring organization, where respect and initiative are grounded in the organization's culture. Moreover, the usage of participatory leadership serves as a motivator to encourage others in the organization to serve the leader. The leader, in turn, receives loyalty and commitment from subordinates; and this, in turn, strengthens and even elevates his or her status as a leader.

Autocratic leadership on the other hand gives leaders the ability to make tough decisions when there is no consensus within the organization. In military organizations, this expectation is institutionalized and expected. In the final analysis, however, whatever decision is made, a leader will always be held accountable and responsible and in some situations may be blamed when problems arise from a bad decision. To lead is to set an example in an organization, and there are always strong expectations to do so. People within the organization expect it, and they want and expect their leader to make the tough decisions, when necessary.

Steps to achieve the ability to practice a flexible combination of the participative and autocratic styles of leadership:

1. Read about different leadership styles (theoretical and what it takes to implement), and understand what differentiates one from another.
   a. Understand those styles that have been successful in the military.
      i. Recognize and comprehend the participatory and autocratic styles of leadership.
      ii. Know when and how to use them.
2. Ascertain through observations the organization's culture and climate and determine what style of leadership would be most effective.
3. If possible, solicit individuals' points of view but be guarded before implementing.
4. Have a good understanding of what motivates individuals in the organization. If it is within your power, motivate them.
   a. Develop a plan with milestones and implement.
5. Read biographies of leaders (successful and not so successful) and see if you can draw any value from their leadership experiences.
6. If in a leadership position, seek feedback from colleagues on your effectiveness.
7. Be honest, be open and ask yourself the question, "What is it about my leadership that I can change to make it more effective?" Or ask trusted colleagues and friends what aspect of yourself you must change to be effective. Make a list of areas of improvement and develop a realistic plan to take the necessary steps to make yourself more effective.

4. Intuition. Leaders must have intuition skills. The ability to sense or recognize what will motivate people or what could happen in a situation is incredibly helpful. Whether people are motivated by financial incentives, career progression, or patriotism, leaders have to be adept to understand people's needs and the factors affecting those needs. This, however, requires unique skills, empathy and background knowledge of behavioral sciences (psychology, sociology, communication skills, culture, and religion, to name a few), and more importantly the talent to use these skills and knowledge.

In military organizations, leaders are confronted with issues of varying degrees of complexities each day. Each issue will require input from individuals with special skills and experiences. As such, a leader must have the ability to quickly determine what is important and what is irrelevant to the issue. With this outlook, a leader operates from a strategic framework to see the challenges his or her organization is facing or will face. And so, the challenge for the leader is to first determine the value of what one is saying, filter the information quickly, and steer the discussion to achieve the organization's mission without actually discouraging people on the team. This is where a leader's instinctive intuition skills come to the fore—analyze the situation quickly, make decisions either to keep the course or change it, and still continue to keep everyone motivated.

Intuition skills come from experience and training. The more experience one has, the more an individual will be able to comprehend what is taking place. One's experience is a life-long learning process of solving problems, building a portfolio of achievements, and, with that, shaping one's ability to discern human behavior. Leaders who have the ability to see what truly motivates people can be immensely successful in leading organizations.

In my military experiences, I have found that the ability to judge accurately the factors that motivate people is incredibly valuable. I have often experienced from some colleagues I have worked with that they would find every excuse available not to respond to an assignment or offer help. They would spend precious minutes, and yes, I have seen on a few occasions, whereby literally precious time has been spent on opaque discourses as to why an assignment is not part of one's duty portfolio. For the most part, they can offer no substantive rationale for not wanting to do the work. While their first response is "This is not in my job description," they in time establish and deservedly earn an uncooperative reputation in the organization.

With time, these individuals become encumbrances within the organization and create barriers for leaders not only to accomplish the mission but also, at times, to undermine it. A leader within every level of the organization must be vigilant for such individuals.

Steps to develop one's instinctive intuition skills:

1. Read and increase background knowledge on what it will take to expand your intuition skills. More specifically, determine the following:
   a. What are the skills necessary to understand and motivate people?
   b. What are the skills necessary to predict how people will behave or react?
2. Read biographies of leaders who have shared their experiences on when they relied on their intuition to make decisions. Determine what was the situation, how was the decision made, and the value from the experience. More importantly, understand the context and how it could be applied if confronted with not a similar situation, but one in which a decision must be made with almost comparable challenges.
3. Broaden work experiences on interacting with individuals having different backgrounds to learn about oneself and others. Also, do the following:
   a. Volunteer for work experiences and training to expand intuition skills.
   b. Be open to accept new ideas.

5. *Teams:* Teams are the essential building blocks for military organizational structures. In today's military, teams are not necessarily limited to individuals from the military but also include civilians from other government agencies and colleagues from partner nations. Understanding how teams work and how to structure a team and motivate them could pay dividends for a leader and the organization.

New recruits into the military are placed into teams from day one. There is the expectation that to succeed one must tolerate and support working with others. With this early exposure to teams, military personnel begin to build on the expectation and faith in the team leader. Even as one moves up the rank, this expectation continues. And as one looks up to the organization as the principal leader, there is hope and belief that the leader will do what is right for the organization. Leaders, on the other hand, must be cognizant of his or her teams' needs and what must be done to fill those needs.

Reflecting on my experiences, teams have been useful to the organizations that I have been associated with. However, its usefulness can only be realized if the leader understands team dynamics and takes advantage of every opportunity to guide the team to achieve the mission. To understand team dynamics, one must be aware of human beings' needs and desires and what will motivate the team members to be innovative and productive. Issues relating to motivating people, establishing performance standards for teams, how to bestow recognition, when to remove individuals from a team that are obstructionists, and finally when to disband a team are key to building productive teams.

A leader's awareness of his or her team's makeup must be deep to understand what will and will not motivate the group as a whole. Without the principal leader's self-assertiveness about the value of teams to the organization, there could potentially be, to some extent, a marginalization of the value of teams, thus undermining the organization's mission. Periodic reviews of a team's efforts are necessary to ensure the mission is being accomplished. If a change is necessary, it must be done with care so as not to undermine the mission.

Steps for building and using teams:

1. Read published words to gain an understanding of the following:
   a. Why are teams necessary?
   b. What constitutes a team?
   c. When should a team be used?

d. How should a team be monitored to ensure its effectiveness?
   e. Find examples of the successful usage of a team and understand the scenario and why it was successful.
2. Determine what nonfinancial things that motivate people?
   a. How can resources be used to train individuals on the value of using a team?
3. Read about what successful leaders have to say about teams.
4. Observe teams already in place and determine what makes some effective and others not effective.
   a. Implement successful ideas, and share them within the organization.
   b. Discontinue using ideas that are not effective.
      i. Inform the team of ineffective ideas.
   c. Be on the lookout for those who do not contribute any value to a team.
      i. When such an individual is identified, counsel, provide training, and monitor. If no improvement, remove him/her from the team.
5. Communicate to others in the organization why teams are of value to the organization.
6. Mentor and support others in the organization about the value of using teams.

6. *Respect for others' point of view, but disagree when necessary.* Leaders should show respect for others' points of view. Respect for other people's points of view is of paramount importance—it helps a leader to maintain his or her credibility to lead in the organization because there is an expectation for them to do so. However, when there is disagreement, it must be made known with all degrees of tact and respectfulness, so as not to undermine a person's character but rather why the point of view does not have any merit. In these situations, the general rule of civility (a form of politeness) is important in criticizing the idea, but not the person. In the military, where one's comportment is always under careful scrutiny, a loss of control can immediately tarnish one's character. Such sharp disagreements can

lead one to say things one would not generally say. Moreover, even a poor choice of words will always be on the record; those words can and will be used against you on another occasion, even years later. The impact on the usage of words not properly thought out can be harmful to one's credibility.

Another underlying principle for respect for another person's point of view is that this guideline allows for one to have more self-control of oneself. Self-control gives one the ability to think clearly and frame one's answers in an argument. Additionally, self-control will help one to win an argument. Occasional pauses will give one the opportunity to critically think about what one will say and strengthen one's advantage to win an argument.

During my service career, I have seen many general officers who have incredible abilities of self-control to show respect to other individuals' points of view. This quality gives one the time to think and deliver their answers with the utmost respect, and that in essence is a fundamental sign of an accomplished leader.

Steps for respecting others' point of view:

1. Solicit input from others in the organization in terms of understanding the value of respecting others' points of view. More specifically, do the following:
    a. Encourage individuals to share their opinions and ideas.
        i. Create an environment in which an intellectual discussion and free exchange of ideas can always be achieved.
        ii. When in agreement, give an individual who shared an insightful idea some credit, but do not show any favoritism to marginalize others in the team.
        iii. When in disagreement, ask for clarification. Do not use words to castigate but rather keep the discussion at an intellectual and civil level.

b. Publicly thank individuals for their input or communicate with a few words in a written note to personally thank them.
c. Maintain an atmosphere for the free exchange of ideas until the internal policy is made.
   i. Even after an internal policy is made, still encourage ideas for revisiting and changing a policy, if necessary.
2. Mentor and support others in the organization about the value of respecting others' points of view.

7. *Show humility.* Humility demonstrates a caring attitude of concern and earnestness of respect. Organizations are made up of people, and people naturally tend to yearn for respect. Leaders who project this attribute—showing respect for others—will quickly earn the respect of others within the organization. And such humility humanizes a leader. Moreover, it gives a leader some opportunities to develop solid relationships based on mutual respect. Yet despite the air force as a military organization, its leaders still need to project a caring demeanor. It is thus likely that not showing a caring demeanor could put at risk a leader's ability to establish strong relationships with others in the organization.

Leaders sometimes have constant or irregular contact and interaction with individuals in the organization. Increasing such contacts help to make one an effective leader. Such contacts and interaction help to facilitate the process to build relationships with others, and it also makes it easier for a leader to establish himself or herself as a caring individual. In return, the leader will be accorded the same respect.

For obvious reasons, the military tends to project a warrior ethos. But even in a war zone, even so, humility is even more critical for interaction for those involved in combat and with the indigenous population. In a combat zone, airmen are under a tremendous amount of stress, and such conditions could affect one's behavior and conduct. Leaders who do not show any concern or project a lack of concern could impact negatively the morale of individuals in the organization. For example, taking no notice or disregarding the emotional issues airmen are likely facing or could potentially face will negatively impact individuals in the organization. An effective leader must be astute to show concern and take an interest in those factors that would potentially impact the morale or the inner health of all those he or she has responsibilities over.

Humility extends from those within the organization even to the indigenous population in a foreign country where the military organization is based. Showing humility gives a leader a tremendous advantage to win over some segments of an indigenous population. For example, in Afghanistan and Iraq, "winning the hearts and minds" of the local population was a matter of much concern and interest. As a result, US military leaders periodically were seen interacting with the indigenous population in order to show sincere concern and humility for the challenges they were facing. In projecting such concern and humility, a leader will show to his or her subordinates a sentiment of caring to win the hearts and minds of the local population, which is key to overseas operations, but this takes time and patience.

Steps for showing humility to others:

1. Recognize and communicate the self-worth of all people (in the organization and the indigenous population in a foreign country).
    a. Understand the theoretical imperatives of human behavior, such as needs and security.
    b. Extend the highest degree possible of respect to everyone in every possible opportunity.
    c. Do not let personal emotions affect your interaction with others.
    d. Use words of positive acknowledgment of your subordinates.
    e. Acknowledge an individual's presence with a few words and with friendly eye contact.

2. Mentor and support others in the organization about the value of respecting others' self-worth.
   a. Communicate the value of the importance of respecting one's self-worth to everyone in the organization.
   b. Put into practice what you communicate.

8. *Ongoing learning program (listen, write, speak, and read).* The learning process never ends, and thus, it must be continuous. An effective leader must have an ongoing learning program to sharpen his or her intellectual abilities and communication skills. It is imperative to stay abreast of current information, issues, and events as this would help one to speak articulately about any issue and make better decisions. Despite one's workload, one must find time to read. In fact, it must be a priority. If it is not, one could become less informed, soon ineffective, and in time irrelevant to the organization.

Reading is perhaps one of the most effective ways for a manageable ongoing learning program. Reading broadens one's perspectives, and it helps to learn about the challenges people face and how to overcome them. For example, prior to entering the Air War College, I read several books, one of which was David McCullough's outstanding work, *1776*.[25] I was amazed about the challenges some of our nation's revolutionary war heroes endured during tremendous personal sacrifices to help win the revolutionary war. Take the story of Mr. Henry Knox, a twenty-five-year-old bookseller from Boston, with his nineteen-year-old brother accompanying him—the initiatives he took to help George Washington to retrieve and move several tons of cannon pieces from Fort Ticonderoga on Lake Champlain in upstate New York to Boston, in the winter, and covering over three hundred miles. To read the story to understand the challenges and see what Mr. Knox accomplished was inspiring; it is the human spirit and ingenuity he used to accomplish this almost impossible goal. One learns from such stories that impossible challenges can be overcome with tenacity and an inner drive. Mr. Knox's accomplish-

---

[25] David McCullough, 1776 (New York: Simon and Schuster, 2005), pp. 59–92.

ment was inspiring not for what he did, but the conditions he had to overcome to achieve his goal, an impossible goal at first thought.

Reading is a matter of great importance to the US Air Force. The chief of staff of the air force publishes a list of recommended books for airmen to read and posted on the air force portal. For those with a hectic schedule, and not knowing what to read, this is a place to begin. An additional source of information to read is the *Early Bird*—summaries of key articles in major newspapers in the United States and available daily to airmen on the air force and other Department of Defense websites, free of charge.

Steps for developing an effective ongoing learning program:

1. With an honest self-assessment, determine one's personal education and communication skill inventory or capability.
    a. Determine what other education credentials or communication skills you must have to be effective in the organization—make a list.
    b. Determine what is doable within the short and long term and the resources needed.
    c. Develop a plan of action to achieve what is doable—implement the plan.
    d. Take advantage of the organization's training program.
2. Regularly read books on a variety of issues and discuss with colleagues.
3. Observe how successful leaders communicate (orally and in writing).
    a. Determine your deficiencies to communicate.
    b. Take the opportunity to improve your weaknesses.
4. Encourage others in the organization about the value of having an ongoing learning program and sharpening one's communication skills.

9. *Understand one's tactical and strategic landscape.* To be effective, one must at all times have a keen understanding of one's organization's tactical and strategic point of view. Even if an organization

does not have a tactical mission, it will still have short-term and long-term objectives. With short-term and long-term objectives come various degrees of dynamic changes that are continuously taking place to shape the landscape. For leaders to be effective, they must frequently communicate their views and ideas within the organization so that everyone can understand the mission and objectives, with respect to where the leader envisions he or she wants to steer the organization.

In the tactical (short-term, could be minutes, hours, days, or several months, depending on the context of the situation) landscape, organizations are faced with time-sensitive mission essential tasks, which are detrimental to the organization's mission. Likewise, for the strategic (long-term, could be a year or several years) landscape, issues on the horizon may be percolating, and those need to be continuously analyzed and developed into plans of action to ensure they do not become a strategic shock.[26] All military organizations are faced with such mission essential challenges, and leaders must have the ability to understand their respective landscapes.

Individuals in an organization need aim points for guidance. To understand one's landscape, a leader must define what the mission and areas of responsibility are so each member sees and understands what needs to be accomplished. An organization's mission must be understandable and transparent for everyone. Thus, a leader must

---

[26] According to the Office of Secretary of Defense (Policy Planning), a strategic shock "is an event that punctuates the evolution of a trend (a discontinuity that either rapidly accelerates its pace or significantly changes its trajectory) and, in so doing, undermines the assumptions on which our current policies are based. Some 'strategic shocks' may not surprise us—we actively plan for them, both to reduce the risk of their occurrence and to be positioned to act. Other 'strategic shocks' may catch us unaware and unprepared. Shocks—or strategic surprises—can change how we think about security and the role of the military. With hindsight, it is clear that most shocks are the product of long-term trends. The challenge is identifying key trends and preadaptation for strategic shocks before they occur." Source: *Air University Research Information System*, accessed on July 26, 2007, from the following Department of Defense intranet website: https://www.afresearch.org/skins/rims/display.aspx?moduleid=be0e99f3-fc56-4ccb-8dfe-6

communicate what it is he or she is responsible for and summarize those objectives into an unambiguous and understandable statement.

Mission statements are unique ways of presenting those aim points, but the statements must be clear, rather than fused with hyperbole and terms that are in vogue. A well-thought-out statement holds countless intrinsic benefits; specifically, it is the visualization of what is important and what must be achieved, but it must be simple and easy to understand, and has some implicit flexibility.

Over the years and especially since I became associated with NATO, I came to understand more and more the importance of the tactical and strategic landscape. Having a well-developed grasp of the US Delegation's mission to NATO helped me to develop an unequivocal understanding of what my role should be. That understanding also helped me to write reports and assessments and communicate ideas consistent with the organization's mission. It became apparent to me it was also my responsibility that the more and more I understood the tactical and strategic landscape, the more I could deliver the products my supervisors needed. Moreover, the more I understood my senior's perspectives, the more I knew what was important and what needed to be done.

At Central Command, I saw firsthand the importance of the value of the tactical and strategic landscape. In command with active ongoing military operations in Afghanistan, it was indeed more important to know the environment and the surrounding areas in which regional cooperation was critical to winning the war on terror. More specifically, with military operations in Afghanistan and Iraq, the command's senior leaders understood the importance of the environment. Through frequent daily meetings with various staff officers from diverse functional areas, they articulated the ideas necessary to persuade individuals to critically think about what is needed to win the war on terror and put in place the mechanisms to help the indigenous population to live a better life. For example, staff officers were tasked to look beyond their areas of responsibility and identify the substantive ideas to change the dynamics in Afghanistan and Iraq so that more normal life for the people could take root.

Whether it was a tactical situation or strategic issue, senior leaders at Central Command seemed to clearly "see" the environment in which they operate. Their views on the situation in Afghanistan were incredibly helpful to understand the factors within and outside the country that will be necessary to defeat the enemy. For me, I found it exceptionally helpful to listen and understand senior officers' perspectives about the battle space and the surrounding environment on which regional security depended.

Steps to understand one's tactical and strategic landscape:

1. Understand the organization's mission.
2. Determine what it is the organization must achieve and why.
    a. What are the factors that could impact the organization's mission? Or what would happen if the mission is not achieved?
3. Determine the tactical (short-term) and strategic (long-term) objectives.
    a. Understand the rationale for tactical and strategic objectives.
4. Determine the power bases (who wields the most power or where the power is concentrated) in the organization.
    a. Determine the communication sources or networks for the issues pertaining to the organization.
    b. Establish links into the communication sources or networks, if practicable.
    c. Regularly discuss, if there is a need to know and with discretion, the important issues for the organization.
    d. Share ideas and information, with the need to know constraints, to colleagues who are in positions of power to get their perspectives.
5. Put oneself in a senior leader's position to determine his or her tactical and strategic objectives from their vantage points.

6. Frequently revisit one's responsibility and see how it fits into the organization's mission.
7. Continuous visualization of what senior leaders have to accomplish and the factors that could potentially impede the success of the mission.
8. Uninterrupted exploration of how the organization is achieving its mission.
   a. If it is not being achieved, what must be done to accomplish it?

10. Character and integrity. Character and integrity are essential elements a leader must have to successfully lead an organization. Character is essentially the quality of one's temperament, moral fiber, and overall nature of a person. On the other hand, integrity implies honesty, truthfulness, and veracity of one's reliability and uprightness. In a high-profile position, a leader is continuously under public scrutiny. The glare of publicity is a manifestation of the public's interest in the military and whether the leader is indeed an exceptional person upon whom trust has been bestowed.

Human nature expects a leader to be an extraordinary person. As such, a leader is expected to have unique skills and unparalleled abilities to motivate people and accomplish things an average person cannot do. With such expectation, a high degree of trust is placed on the leader. While a leader's skills and abilities are unique in a way, an average person, on the other hand, does not have such skills and abilities a leader has. Unquestionably, a leader will appear as one who embodies unique characteristics and as one from whom much is expected.

In my interaction with leaders in the military, I have had the belief that each had a pristine character. The idea that a leader is expected to direct an organization also includes a characterization that the leader must have the moral character to continuously set an example where no doubt is ever placed on his or her integrity. Such a leader projects an ability to be fair, one with wisdom and a unique ability to judge and make decisions with tremendous confidence. People by their nature want a leader to have such uniqueness.

Throughout my military career, I have found that effective leaders with whom I have the privilege to interact embody such unique characters that seem to naturally sparkle. When a leader casts such positive attributes, it encourages and motivates individuals to conduct themselves in a manner that helps the leader to accomplish the mission.

Integrity is an extra special attribute with absolute significance, and it manifests itself at all times. One expects a leader to be honest and truthful. But it is also likely for one to be placed in a leadership position if one is not honest and truthful. In such situations, such leaders will lose all credibility when internal conflicts compound from the lack of ability to deal with organizational issues. I am convinced the military leaders I have interacted with were honest and truthful; it is just inconceivable for one to be otherwise in order to achieve the rank they have attained. A military leader making decisions to impact people's lives and spend taxpayers' money must have confidence in all those he or she is interacting with. One with high-quality integrity generally can expect others' support; however, one with a tarnished integrity can most of the time expect no support.

The issue of character and integrity is a recurring theme for effective leadership. Throughout my career, I have tried to understand each leader's character and integrity that I interacted with. I have found high-ranking leaders' characters and integrity are fundamental distinctiveness that made them what they are. The leaders generally seemed to have high moral personal standards and projected an atmosphere of honesty consistent with the US Air Force's values on what it expects its leaders and all its airmen to be.

Steps for strengthening one's character and integrity:

1. Determine what is and what is not acceptable in the organization.
    a. Use the knowledge to shape or modify one's character and integrity to what is acceptable in the organization.
2. Change or modify one's behavior to what is accepted.
3. Conduct oneself within norms of acceptable comportment.

4. Be honest in interaction with colleagues.
5. Keep one's word; do what you say you will do.
6. Keep a promise. If, however, it is not possible to keep, then apologize as soon as practicable.
7. Always treat everyone with respect.
8. Accept responsibility when a mistake is made and learn from the mistake.
9. Set an example as one with pristine character and integrity.
10. Show a willingness to accept new ideas that could change an organization.

11. Perpetual self-analysis. Self-analysis allows one to reflect on one's actions and to identify weaknesses and strengths. This personal evaluation gives one a deeper insight into one's actions and how one can improve one's image and abilities. The ability of anyone to do some self-analysis is a mind and willpower introspection that one can use to determine his or her strengths and weaknesses. This inward searching to explore one's inner self, to see and learn what one does wrong or what one must do to improve one's skills and capabilities, is incredibly important and helpful. Effective leaders accomplish this naturally. Anyone with the ability to do such self-analysis can embark on the road to be a successful leader.

Relentless self-analysis gives one the ability to really look deeply at one's self. To explore one's inner thoughts and ask the question, "What do I need to do to be an effective and successful leader?" is powerful and the beginning to identify weaknesses that must be changed. But the ability to ask the question requires first for the individual to be willing to self-critique and identify those areas in which one can improve. Without the ability to admit one has made a mistake, the self-analysis process will be meaningless. It is indeed more than asking the question, it is the follow-through with a personal development plan to make the changes and compromises and do what is necessary to achieve the goal to be an effective and successful leader, which really matters.

It is often said that one learns from one's mistakes. However, it is one's willingness to first admit to making a mistake that gives one an internal nudge to appraise what went wrong. The admitting of making a mistake provides for personal accountability over one's behavior, which is a compelling force not many people have or that some people are unwilling to even consider. To some degree, enlightened individuals easily admit to a mistake, learn from the mistake, and take the necessary action to change or modify one's behavior. Others, however, are unwilling to accept such shortcomings as personal imperfections.

My personal philosophical approach to self-analysis is that it must be conducted with some degree of honesty. Self-searching and admitting to a mistake, apologize sincerely for it, when warranted, has huge benefits. It provides immediate personal relief and opportunities for strengthening one's relationship with another. However, few people can admit or are willing to admit to making a mistake.

Self-analysis is more than a self-critique of one's personal mistakes; it's about respecting others' ideas. One's self-analysis helps to strengthen trust with others, by acknowledging one's mistakes and taking steps for redemption. It is not the acknowledgment; rather, it is the change in behavior or one's attitudes that are crucial.

In my observation of leaders, I sometimes saw clues or indications that a leader has performed some self-analysis. Effective leaders generally would humbly say, "In retrospect, I should have done...," or "I have learned over the years that...," or "Past experience showed that..." It is through these deliberations that self-analysis is occurring and individuals are deciding what is it they need to do to be an effective leader, and it is from these examples that we learn.

Steps to develop a self-analysis program to identify weaknesses:

1. Recognize and admit that one must have an open mind and change must come from within.
2. Accept that the key to identifying one's weaknesses begins with the willingness to ask oneself the question, "What do I need to do to be an effective and successful leader?"
    a. Be objective. List all the items for improvement. Determine what is doable and implement.

3. Ask colleagues and friends what your weaknesses are?
   a. Solicit their recommendations or ideas on how to turn the weaknesses into strengths.
4. For each weakness, list what it is that you must do for improvement.
   a. Develop a plan of action with a milestone for each item.
   b. Implement the plan and stick to it.
5. Make the self-analysis a significant daily event.
   a. Possibly at the end of the day, ask yourself what you did right and what you did not so well.
   b. For each item that was not done as well, determine the cause of the problem and what is required to fix it.
6. Be honest about your weaknesses and establish a willingness to change.

Reflections on Succeeding in the Mission

Success is more than accomplishing one's mission. It is rather a selfless endeavor in which one inspires his or her team to give more than what is expected, to accomplish one's organization's mission. Military culture service instills upon each member what is expected to accomplish one's duty, with no expectation of personal pursuit of recognition. So to be really successful to accomplish one's mission, one must think and take the initiative to perform the absolute best possible and always give more than what is expected.

For leaders to be effective, they also need to inspire individuals to think about performing at a level beyond what is expected. Leaders can motivate to a point, but it is the enlightened and free-thinking person who will take the initiative to pursue the right skills to achieve extraordinary things beyond what is expected for the organization. Such individuals continuously seek opportunities for self-improvement to sharpen their skills and abilities. A successful leader must understand the environment in which he or she operates and seize every chance to motivate all individuals to grab opportunities necessary for self-improvements.

UNCOMMON DUTIES IN THE UNITED STATES AIR FORCE

I have often found in the military most tasks are generally straightforward. Whether it is planning for an operation or preparing a document for policy consideration, one generally obtains either oral or written instructions on what is required. The military provides the training to do what is required, and through continuous work assignments, individuals learn the procedures necessary to complete any assigned task. However, it is the airman who takes the initiative to always sharpen his or her skills and abilities that ends up more likely to succeed. Such an individual projects a positive image that creates an atmosphere attracting others for a collegiate team with a better focus on accomplishing the mission.

Effective leaders want their staff to be successful in performing all their tasks. They generally give specific instructions on what is expected from each task. There are times, however, when leaders do not give specific instructions; it is then left to one's initiative and creativity to understand what the task is and what is expected. In these circumstances, it is the employee with broad imagination who can see what is required for success.

On many occasions, I have observed colleagues lacking the personal drive to think deeply of their responsibilities. These individuals just do the basic task and nothing more. One must anticipate what a leader needs and provide the products that will exceed the leader's expectations, even if the initial instructions did not ask for it. Leaders expect employees to take the initiative and do what is necessary to achieve their organization's mission. Thus, every employee, once in a while, must try to understand a leader's perspective from that leader's vantage point and most times must put oneself in a leader's position and visualize what the leader is responsible for and why.

It is expected for individuals in the military to succeed in his or her task. Being successful, on the other hand, is a different matter. But being successful, however, is a higher form of succeeding. It is one in which one must always seek delivery of quality products that exceed expectations. To anticipate what a leader need is really to think like a leader and deliver products that would answer almost every possible question, in any possible scenario. In actuality, one must aspire to be successful and deliver more than what is required. Not thinking about being successful would undermine one's full potential and the organization's mission.

On Success

This section will discuss key attributes to succeed in one's mission. While there are numerous attributes, I have found there are specific qualities to make one successful. The most substantive ones are discussed below:

1. *Continuous self-reflection*—"What do I need to do to excel at what I do?" To succeed, one must continuously self-reflect. The self-reflection must be focused on determining what aspects of one's behavior and attitudes must be changed in order to do what is right to be successful. Changing one's behavior is an extremely complicated personal matter, and it requires the willpower and motivation to initiate a self-reflection process. While such a process is personal, only those individuals who clearly have the ability to ask themselves the question and follow through to do what is necessary can successfully self-reflect. This process must be honest to think over deeply about one's strengths and weaknesses and then focus on those areas for improvement.

An enlightened individual is one who seeks ways to improve one's approach and who will ask oneself, "What do I need to do to excel at what I do?" While asking the question is a major personal hurdle to overcome, it is indeed the first step in the process to excel. On the other hand, the lack of personal initiative to embrace ideas of excellence would be a barrier in the self-reflection process.

It is more than asking the self-reflection question. It is the ability to think really deeply and examine one's personal weaknesses, strengths, inhibitions, and ability or capability to admit that one must make changes necessary to excel that really matters. A sincere self-reflection is absolutely essential as it will provide one with critical information on how to constructively transform oneself to achieve at a higher performance level.

During my duty assignments at NATO and Central Command, I had numerous assignments to prepare written products for senior officers, including generals and high-ranking civilians and ambassadors. Seeing these individuals interact in meetings, it was easy for me to determine what was needed. Sometimes, doing just the bare minimum was an option, but never a good idea to take such an approach. Such an attitude will always have a negative impact on one's reputation. I understood the mission and what the leaders required, and I did everything within my scope of responsibilities and especially those within my discretion to prepare products beyond the minimum expectations. It was through this approach leaders notice and had the confidence in me to support them in their respective mission.

There are individuals who are satisfied with always doing the absolute minimum amount of work. The risk here is that these individuals can endanger their organization and, in doing so, negatively impact their own reputation. On the other hand, there are individuals who perform more than the normal expectation of what is required and very quickly become extremely valuable to an organization—and I have had the privilege to interact with such individuals. It is the latter group of individuals (forward-thinking and with a positive attitude) who make the greatest impact on an organization.

Steps to develop a continuous self-reflection program:

1. Acknowledge that the keys to excellence are within reach.
2. Understand that to excel will require a willingness to change one's behavior.
3. One must be willing to ask oneself, "What do I need to do to excel at what I do?"
4. Read about successful individuals and study what their characteristics and personalities are.
    a. Identify those attributes you can accept and within your capabilities to implement.
5. Ask colleagues and friends what are your strengths and weaknesses.
    a. Have an open mind and be willing to accept criticism.

6. Design a plan to implement the positive items from successful leaders and change negative aspects of one's behavior. Put the plan into action.
   a. Establish realistic timelines.
   b. Do periodic reviews to determine if one is achieving what you set out to do?

2. No conflict with personal philosophical beliefs and an organization's mission. A divergence between one's philosophical beliefs with respect to an organization's mission will impact whether or not one is successful in an organization. Leaders take attention to detail and the precision of their mission statements' narrative to show the scope of what they want to be accomplished. With that, there are implicit expectations that employees must be conscientious in their efforts to achieve the goals and objectives set forth. Employees are thus faced with the choice; either one supports the mission wholeheartedly or not. Those who give total support and excel will find that success in the organization is assured; those who do not would inevitably put their career at risk.

To believe in an organization's mission does not necessarily imply that one gives up one's identity to become totally subordinate to the organization. To believe in the mission will make it easier to accomplish the mission. On the contrary, this is only about the belief in the organization's mission and doing everything possible so the organization can accomplish its mission. A consistent demonstration of strong philosophical beliefs to implement an organization's goals and objectives projects a positive attitude to strengthen professional relationships with other colleagues. And it is the strong professional relationships that one can build upon and take advantage of to do what is necessary for the organization's benefit. Demonstrating inconsistent points of view with what key leaders believe could potentially undermine an organization's mission.

Additionally, having strong and positive philosophical views about an organization does not necessarily mean that one must engage in groupthink, agreeing and making decisions collectively as a group. Indeed, it is quite the opposite. In the air force, I have found as I moved up the ranks, it was even more important for everyone to think independently about issues and offer ideas to fix a problem, even if the ideas are not within the consensus of the majority. At Central Command, I have found that senior leaders do ask the staff direct questions to solicit their ideas. Not only did the command's leaders want the unconventional thoughts that provoke discussions in the search for proposals that fix a problem, but also it was, I believe, a subtle way to ensure the organization's culture produces internal discussions to generate great ideas.

My experiences have shown that individuals whose views are limited in scope tend to do the minimum. These individuals are more apt to agree with others or be dismissive of unconventional ideas. Moreover, these individuals have a tendency and predisposition to have negative views about the senior leaders who are forward-thinking and who demand more from everyone. Essentially, these individuals are not productive. I have also found that those who have strong philosophical and positive views about the organization will have the confidence of their leaders. Such individuals will do what is necessary to accomplish the organization's mission.

Steps to ensure that there are no conflicts with personal philosophical beliefs and an organization's mission:

1. Read the organization's mission statement.
    a. Seek an understanding of what the organization wants to achieve and how it plans to achieve it.
    b. Determine the organization's expectation of its employees with respect to accomplishing its mission.
2. Reevaluate one's philosophical beliefs with that of the organization's mission.
    a. Are there conflicts? If yes, determine what they are.
    b. Evaluate each conflict to determine whether one can make a compromise to accept the organization's mission as it is.

      c. If one cannot make a compromise, then it would be advisable to leave the organization and seek employment elsewhere.
3. Perform frequent personal assessments of philosophical beliefs with the organization's mission to determine if there are any conflicts or potential for conflicts.
4. Make sure that one's philosophical beliefs and the organization's mission are compatible.

3. Character and integrity: A pristine character and integrity are vital for success in any organization. One's character and integrity present an image with which one is judged. Perceptions of others are established and influenced by such an image. Individuals in positions of power are easily influenced by their own perceptions, and sometimes, it is difficult to change those perceptions. Thus, it becomes more important for those who want to excel to be extremely cognizant of one's behavior and wary of the implications of one's actions.

One's personal activities (private and public) and even demeanor tend to shape one's character and integrity. People generally are invariably under constant close watch (not necessarily, surreptitiously) by colleagues and individuals in an organization. Thus, it is even more important to manage one's activities to present a positive image within the parameters of organizational culture for acceptable behavior. This awareness comes with some degree of maturity and personal self-control to make sure that one's actions do not negatively impact one's character and integrity.

One's character and integrity are crucial for the organization's cohesiveness. In fact, most jobs in the military require a security clearance, and thus, each individual is required to maintain an unblemished character and integrity. When one does something to tarnish his or her character, it poses a risk not only to themselves but also to the entire organization and its mission. Senior leaders always respond vigorously to do whatever is necessary to protect the integrity and reputation of the institution. Indeed, some leaders are empathetic and have wide discretion of power to interpret facts and would tend to give someone a second chance. But one cannot presuppose that a leader will use his or her discretion to help, but rather always cognizant that the leader will always first protect the integrity and reputation of the organization. One with an unblemished character and integrity, who makes an honest mistake, is more likely to have a second chance. However, one with borderline character and integrity would encounter difficulty getting a second chance. As a result, the rationale for maintaining a positive character and integrity is absolutely crucial.

My military experiences have shown that character and integrity are absolutely critical to maintain the confidence of senior officials I reported to. The more pristine one's character and integrity are, the more trust is placed on the individual. But trust is fragile and not necessarily guaranteed. Once one's trust is lost, one's career and reputation could be tainted and most times almost impossible to regain. Consequently, maintaining a vigorous oversight to manage one's character and integrity will ensure that one will have an open pathway for success in the organization.

Steps to develop and maintain one's character and integrity:

1. Conduct a personal assessment of the organizational culture to determine what is acceptable and what is not.
2. Perform an honest evaluation of one's character and integrity to determine areas for improvement.
   a. Make a list and determine the extent to which one is willing to make substantive changes.
3. Evaluate successful and not so successful leaders and determine the foundations of their attitudes for character and integrity.
   a. Determine which attributes you are willing to accept.
   b. Decide to what extent you would change certain aspects of your character to fit what is expected in the organizational culture.
4. Establish quality personal standards of conduct to strengthen one's character and integrity.

5. Manage your activities so as not to tarnish your character and integrity.
6. Be honest, keep your word, and deliver what you promise you will do.

4. Sharpen communication skills: The key to success is superb communications skills. Communication is a priceless ability, and it can be learned. The ability to listen more, write well, and speak less is without a doubt the tool one must have to convey ideas, thoughts, and solutions to problems. In all organizations, it is the diffusion of innovative ideas that gets senior leaders' attention. Senior leaders are constantly confronted with complex challenges, and they need professional opinions and judgments on how to resolve the issues they face. Those who can articulate ideas and defend those ideas with civility will get the attention of individuals in positions of power in the organization.

Words are powerful. They do matter and can influence and change people's opinions. The ability to deliver the words is incredibly important to succeed in everything that one does. This eloquence—the ability to deliver precise words—is critical for all organizations and even more so in the military. In the military where the giving of orders (oral and written) is the norm, the ability to use the English language, choose the right words, and deliver those words to a variety of people from different backgrounds (and varying work motivation and work ethic) is an extraordinary skill. Words influence people, especially leaders. The key is the ability to persuade and ensure that precise instructions are given for specific tasks.

Information and ideas are the lifeblood of a successful organization. With the introduction of the Internet and the ability to transmit messages (emails), the flow of information has increased exponentially. Now with the increased volume of information comes the need to make sure one's communication is precise and to the point for leaders who have less and less time to manage their intake of electronic information and also in the interchange of information orally to individuals in the organization.

The skill to communicate requires more than just delivering ideas. It is also one of being respectful of other peoples' opinions and one's self-control to manage one's desire or willingness to communicate. Being indifferent to other people can result in losing their interest and respect. In my military experiences, I interacted with some individuals (no general officers in this category) who would give extended dissertations on issues, with no substance at all. They spoke to impress others about what they knew and with a domineering attitude to project intellectual superiority. These individuals generally never gain the respect of their colleagues and subordinates.

On the other hand, I have met exceptional individuals who were incredibly eloquent. They delivered ideas with such preciseness that it was easy to see the ideas they intended to articulate. I remember one general officer at Central Command who spoke with such preciseness that each time he spoke, he immediately got the attention and respect to which he was entitled, not necessarily because of his rank, but of what he was saying and his tone of delivery. He chose his words carefully and delivered them with confidence. Moreover, his written communications were magnificently crafted, with language to show eloquence and preciseness. It was my interaction with this officer that further reinforced the value of superb communication skills.

Steps to sharpen communication skills:

1. Perform a personal assessment of your communication skills (listening, speaking, and writing).
2. Solicit colleagues and friends for a sincere assessment of your communication skills.
   a. Determine strengths and weaknesses.
   b. For each weakness, determine what must be done to change weaknesses into strengths, and develop a plan of action. Implement the plan of action.
3. Conduct periodic observations of those with communication skills and determine what they do very well.

4. Take advantage of every training opportunity to improve communication skills.
5. Implement a rigorous personal reading program to broaden the command of the English language and thinking abilities.
6. Volunteer for opportunities to use all your communication skills.

5. Broaden practical experiences. One must broaden one's foundation of educational and practical experiences to excel in one's profession. Doing a job really well within acceptable limits is expected; but to excel, one must seek to continuously expand one's background knowledge beyond the day-to-day activities and use that knowledge for the benefit of the organization. It is common today for job responsibilities to overlap functional and technical subject matter. Thus, some knowledge in as many subjects as possible will be of advantage to articulate issues and offer substantive recommendations during any discussion.

In today's dynamic environment, individuals are expected to work in teams to solve complex problems that extend beyond one specific functional area. A team can only be effective if its members have some knowledge to contribute and the motivation to participate to accomplish the team's charge. As such, the more background knowledge one has and the more one is willing to be an active participant, the more one is of value. Also, in today's environment, one is expected to work independently on issues of major importance that cross-functional topics. Whether one is in a team or is working independently, it is the one with the most extensive background knowledge who will be in the best position to contribute the most to the mission.

In assignments at NATO and at Central Command, I have found that one must have diverse educational and work experiences to be effective. As an intelligence planner, the more experience I had on a particular topic and peripheral areas, the easier it was to discuss complex issues with senior officials. Moreover, I found that the more knowledge one has and the more one can engage in substantive discussions in a respectful manner, the more respect one will receive. Along with the respect, one achieves some degree of integrity with senior officials. More specifically at Central Command, as I interacted with many individuals (senior and midlevel), it became more apparent that the more I contributed in a respectful manner, the more credibility I seem to have attained. For example, on issues relating to the US/Pakistan partnership, in one week, I participated in substantive discussions along with many colleagues within Central Command and other agencies on matters relating to internally displaced persons, Congressional funding procedures, exploring the possibility of building a railroad, attributes of geographical terrain, managing security cooperation programs (foreign military sales), strategic communications, and oversight for Congressional funding programs, to name a few. Being attentive and having a clear grasp of the dynamics of the meetings and teams, I came to recognize that some individuals rely on others to think. Consequently, the ones with the broadest background knowledge who contribute quickly in a respectful manner seem to have a clear advantage over others to excel. Thus, for individuals who have taken the initiative to broaden his or her background knowledge, opportunities to excel in the organization will be assured.

Steps to broaden one's educational and practical experiences:

1. Conduct a personal assessment of your educational and practical experiences.
    a. Determine how you rank with other colleagues.
    b. Decide what your deficiencies are and what areas need to be strengthened.
2. Evaluate your personal continuing education plan.
    a. If none, establish one.
    b. If you have one, then is it effective to broaden your background knowledge and practical experiences?
        i. If no, then make the necessary changes to make it effective.

3. Ask reporting officials, colleagues, and friends what is it you need to broaden your educational and practical experiences and incorporate this knowledge into your personal continuing education plan.
4. Set personal goals and timelines within your personal continuing education plan.
   a. Make sure your continuing education plan does not conflict with the mission of your organization.
   b. Do periodic reviews of your continuing education plan to make sure you are achieving objectives to benefit you and the organization.

6. *Reading:* Reading broadens the mind. Most importantly, it helps one to build up an arsenal of ideas, ready for usage at any moment's notice, especially when working on issues of national importance. In the military, ideas are continuously needed to develop plans and strategies for commanders. Individuals must present ideas for various groupings with colleagues and senior leaders and also be able to communicate those ideas with persuasiveness and confidence to show one's knowledge of the subject matter. This skill to develop and communicate ideas with compelling persuasiveness comes from a personal commitment to continuous improvement of one's mind and knowledge base. Of greatest importance, it is the practice of reading that does just that.

Reading also develops our abilities to apply knowledge in circumstances that are, by their nature, professionally competitive. Substantiated facts and data and an insightful perspective become useful in brainstorming sessions to find preeminent concepts for problems. The question that should be asked is "How does one become more knowledgeable?" It is really through continual exposure to facts and data from an array of sources and the ability to distinguish what is accurate or what is not. Reading opens one to different perspectives and information from unusual points of view. It is through exposure to these diverse sources of information that one becomes more enlightened and has the ability to make a distinction between fact and misinformation. Reading also gives one the ability to eloquently describe with justifiable passion ideas in simple words and with the spontaneity of thought.

To lead, one must have access to a broad spectrum of information and from different sources, as possible. Gifted leaders have vast knowledge bases to tap into at any moment's notice. In my interaction with many senior leaders, it is clear these individuals have a natural ability to think and quickly use the right words and facts to communicate. Their knowledge base must be constantly replenished, and it is only by the habit of reading this is achieved. Without exposure to information of value, one places oneself at a disadvantage and potentially putting one's value as a leader at risk.

The decision on whether to read is personal, and the value of doing so is infinite to excel. On the other hand, not having an individual reading program increases the risk of one becoming irrelevant to one's organization.

Steps to establishing a personal reading program:

1. Ask yourself the question, "When was the last time I read a book or article?"
   a. If the answer to the question is a long time ago, then you need to read more.
2. You must accept and believe in the idea that reading broadens the mind.
   a. If you do not believe that reading broadens the mind, then reading would not matter.
3. Read some military biographies of senior military officers and learn what they have to say about the value of reading.
4. Just read and keep on reading, and make it a routine habit.

7. *Understand your surroundings:* One must know one's organization thoroughly to excel. Without a comprehensive understanding of the organization's mission, the power bases (the key leaders and their respective responsibilities), and the climate and culture that permeate every administrative unit, one will put oneself within precarious limits for excellence. An understanding of one's surroundings

and, for that matter, some degree of knowledge of what motivates senior leaders, what they want to achieve, and the challenges they are facing and will face is a key element to excel.

An organization has specific characteristics and needs that are imperative for its success. While some leaders tend to articulate some aspects of the characteristics and needs, others do not because they do not see the importance of doing so. Furthermore, while some leaders communicate their vision of where they want to steer their organizations and the challenges they are facing or will face, others do not because they do not see what to do. For individuals who are in situations with either of these scenarios, it is incumbent to actively search for a deeper understanding of his or her organization. Everything that makes up an organization—what makes it functions, the challenges it is facing, and its needs—must be understood at all times. Not having an interest in these matters will place one at a disadvantage, in which the lack of knowledge will engender a lack of motivation and initiative. In such a case, one will drift into a deepening malaise whereby positive attitudes required for success are wiped out from the individual's consciousness.

Understanding the challenges an organization faces is valuable. The more one knows about an organization, the more valuable one becomes to the team. But the knowledge must be shared with others in the organization for one to be valuable. However, acquiring the knowledge requires a continuous process to scrutinize and search for all aspects of the organization's structure and mission. Incessant and never-ending exploration will give one insight into the challenges and hopefully the courage to share forward ideas with senior leaders to mitigate the challenges.

I have learned the importance to understand everything, to the extent possible, about the challenges organizations' leaders face. The more I knew about the environment and the state of affairs, the more quality products I prepared. At Central Command, on issues about Pakistan, my persistent inquiry into the partnership between the United States and Pakistan guided me to analyze issues in a more critical way, which I deemed were important to senior military officers. Relentless inquiry into my surroundings, what are the factors that influence it, and what was it my commanders wanted to accomplish helped me immensely to deliver quality products to my senior officer—it is this attribute that I am convinced is indispensable to excel in an organization.

Steps to understand one's surroundings:

1. Study your organizational structure.
    a. Determine who are in positions of power, their responsibilities, their mission, and what products must flow to them.
    b. When possible and practicable, provide an opportunity to speak to each individual in a position of power to determine their frame of thinking and their philosophical approach to organizational issues.
2. Determine your role (and importance) in the organization, your mission, and your work products and to whom.
3. Establish a personal plan to complete and present all deliverables on time.
    a. Make sure all work products meet and exceed the customer's expectations.

8. *Initiative:* Leaders are inspired by individuals who take the initiative. Such individuals develop a resourceful attitude to accomplish what really matters for the organization. Undoubtedly, organizations need individuals who take the initiative to perform essential tasks or prepare important products that are not necessarily asked for but essential to accomplish the mission. One's initiative to anticipate what a leader wants will indeed project an optimistic attitude for success, and it is such an approach that creates opportunities to excel.

Leaders have missions of major importance and consequence. Their time is valuable, and with that, perceptive members of the organization must be totally cognizant of what is important and what is not and what must be accomplished. An organization cannot necessarily be effective if its leaders must continuously assign tasks and manage every key element for each task. This is overwhelming, and it decreases morale. Individuals who are keen to notice what is important and deliver the appropriate product will strengthen his or her reputation with respect to allegiance and fidelity to the organization's mission.

One's ability to take the initiative is totally within one's personal control. Without the self-control or imagination to understand what is important for a leader, an individual could in fact develop the reputation as one who engenders a poor work ethic. Such a reputation, obviously, would create impediments to success. While personal success should not be one's overall ulterior motive, it is success for the benefit of the organization that drives initiative and inspire others to do likewise.

Throughout my military career, I found that initiative is a deciding factor for success. Those with a reputation for doing just the bare minimum and nothing else carry a stigma as uninterested and unconcerned individuals. In such a scenario, an individual's career will languish. I have also found that taking the initiative creates an optimistic impression as one who is dependable, conscientious, and reliable. For leaders with complex missions, employees with such characteristics are indispensable and an asset to the organization and will be recognized in due course for accomplishments beyond what is expected.

Steps on taking the initiative:

1. Ask yourself the question, "Do I take the initiative or volunteer for work activities?"
    a. If not, then begin to take the initiative and volunteer for actions that involve work.
2. Observe successful individuals and determine whether they take the initiative or volunteer for activities that involve work.
    a. For those who do not take the initiative, assess their character and reputation within the organization.
        i. If the individual has a poor reputation, ask yourself the question, "Would I want to have that reputation?"

3. Always do more (but do not compromise quality) than what is expected.
4. Continuously strive to maintain the reputation as one who can always be counted on.

9. Establish personal professionalism standards: A well-mannered and respectful approach to others is absolutely necessary for success. In organizations where there are continuous interactions between senior leaders, colleagues, and customers, there is the expectation that one must have the comportment for cordial relationships. Without the extension of good manners during interaction with others, one will put at risk the benefit of that relationship and, most importantly, one's reputation. The risk of tarnishing one's reputation will definitely impact one's potential to succeed in the organization, and once tarnished, it can be virtually impossible to recover it.

People expect to be treated fairly and with respect. In a professional environment, it is only natural for everyone to demonstrate the decorum of civility and respect the self-worth of each person. For some people, the etiquette of civility is an instinctive and common sense approach when interacting with others, even in situations of stress. On the other hand, for others, good manners and consideration are not necessarily innate practices, and for the most part, it is generally a routine custom to be insensitive to others. It is rather, however, a reflexive attitude in which a lack of knowledge, perception, and unwillingness to respect others are common attributes that make up the individual. In essence, the key to success is thus within individuals themselves. And for those individuals who have the ability to be aware of other people's needs and their sensitivities and put in practice a consistent decorum of civility toward other people will, in turn, earn the respect of others and build a base for success.

I have oftentimes seen that successful military leaders project a consistent courteous approach. This approach builds trust and partnerships. To do otherwise would essentially affect a leader's integrity and diminish one's effectiveness. It was clear throughout my military career that successful leaders are aware of the importance to be respectful. They seem to consistently project their personal belief to be respectful in their interaction with others. Frequently, it became noticeable that individuals who had a positive experience with a senior leader would react with a feeling of being a valued member of the organization and, in some respects, be more motivated to work to achieve the organization's mission. Through these observations, I learned the importance of a courteous approach when interacting with others.

My assignment at Central Command was a profound learning experience, which I will cherish for years to come. There, I interacted with individuals who were well-mannered and a few that were not. This experience has given me a rich insight into techniques to interact with individuals in incredible positions of power. Specifically, I learned what was effective to build and strengthen successful partnerships to accomplish the mission. Those who I interacted with and who were well-mannered earned my respect. On the other hand, with those who were not, the relationship on my part was cordial and very rarely extended beyond the issue that was being discussed. On most occasions, individuals who seemed to have something substantive to say did not get a chance to speak. Sometimes, these situations were just frustrating to bear. It is through these experiences that I was convinced a well-mannered and respectful approach will lead to successful professional relationships with individuals and in turn will provide the experience necessary for one's success in the organization.

Steps to establish personal professionalism standards:

1. Evaluate the organizational culture and determine what is acceptable and what is not.
2. Perform a personal assessment of your behavior as you are perceived within the organization. Determine what must be changed to meet what is expected in the organization and implement.
3. Ask reporting officials (if practicable), colleagues, and friends for feedback on your demeanor. Use the feedback to change behavior to meet senior leaders' expectations.

4. Be honest, take an inward thoughtful examination of one's approach to other individuals, and determine whether that approach is respectful to the self-worth of others. If not, then decide on whether you are willing to change or modify your behavior. If yes, then change it.
5. Institute personal self-control so as not to be seen as distasteful, domineering, or pompous. Observe and see what is acceptable for success and decide whether you are willing to change to show a respectful attitude.
6. Never be complacent; instead, show a positive outlook with an open enthusiasm to learn and be of value to one's organization.
7. Be consistent in treating all individuals with respect and for their self-worth as human beings.
8. Focus on the mission with an enthusiastic passion to achieve results that are of value to the organization.

PART III

Introspective Thoughts on the United States Air Force Culture

Since its founding on September 18, 1947, the US Air Force's culture has evolved into distinct organizational subtleties. That now is synonymous with what the USAF is and known to many current and retired airmen for what it is. This culture—for example, its mission, expectations, how things work, and communication through the units and between senior and lower-ranking airmen—will continue to change, as society undergoes change itself. The culture's uniqueness is due in large part to its air force's mission, size, sophisticated resources in its inventory, the unique skills that airmen must have, and the camaraderie between all airmen, current and retired. Additionally, outside forces such as the public's perception of what the air force is and what it has to do in the defense of the nation have kept the public's aura of the airmen's expectation with high esteem. This expectation and the responsibility to defend the United States' worldwide interests will continue to shape the air force's culture.

It is important to understand how and what influences airmen and the air force as an organization and why? The establishment of the United States Space Force on December 20, 2019, will also have an impact on the air force organizational culture because of new mission requirements, technical knowledge requirements for airmen, and the public's expectation and fascination of the airmen who will be protecting the country's space assets, the new, and ultimate frontier.

After the Second World War, relations between the United States and the Soviet Union were tense. The Soviet Union was determined to spread its communist ideology through brute force and proxies, such as supporting legitimate communist parties, unlawful communist movements, and paramilitary organizations throughout the world. Then protecting America's and allied airspace required vast resources and highly trained individuals to quickly respond to foreign threats and maintain the technological advantage at all times. As aviation engineering became more sophisticated in Western and communist countries, the urgency to use the most advanced technology was more critical to maintain the technological edge. The ability to respond to threats decisively was critical, and it is still so today. Indeed, as technology mushroomed over the decades since September 1947, the USAF's mission and complexity expanded. Now the mission is broader, to include space and cyberspace, but still with the focus to *fly, fight, and win*,[27] and maintain air, cyberspace, and space dominance. As the mission evolved and expanded over the years, the organizational culture and expectations shaped how the air force leadership expected airmen to perform their duty.

The air force has successfully protected America's and its allies' airspace since its establishment. From 1947 to today, the air force endured and became a critical institution in the nation's defense array of networks. Airmen, throughout the period, did extraordinary things (some as fighter aces and some on extended flying missions) in the call of one's duty. The elapsed time of history, spanning over seventy years, from the Cold War to an era of space and Internet technology today, required professional forward-thinking leaders with insight to adjust the strategy for complex missions. As such, the air force tradition and practices of accomplishing its mission have institutionalized those activities and traditions as a way of life. Accordingly, this is the spirit of the air force culture as it is today.

It is the airmen who have had the greatest impact on the air force culture. Airmen from every state in the union brought their individual, local, special, and even distinctive knowledge and skills (even idiosyncrasies) with them when they joined the air force. These airmen, though few in numbers when compared to the other service branches, blended together during training and when on duty

---

[27] The United States Air Force Web Portal, retrieved on October 10, 2009, https://www.my.af.mil.

worked as a team to execute the air force mission. When on duty in the homeland or overseas as well, airmen took charge and performed within rules and regulations to accomplish complex missions. Over time, airmen created and refined the culture (integrity, service, and excellence). The attribute, integrity, service, and excellence are key components to keep sophisticated equipment mission-ready.

The air force's mission from its beginning then was to protect the integrity of America's and allied airspace. Today, the mission is still the same, but the tools to do it have increased in sophistication. It is common to see young airmen, with one or more years of service, having incredible responsibilities operating unbelievably sophisticated equipment at ease in their everyday job. This trend will continue, and the demand for more and more information, requiring critical thinking in packaging, will increase the workload on every airman. Senior leaders must be prepared and must be willing to take the initiative to guide and provide the training for all airmen to meet this astounding challenge. Further, new and bold ideas will be needed, and leaders must take initiative to do things across all functional areas to keep airmen motivated and trained to do their mission as effectively as possible. Here are areas for renewed focus:

Resources and oversight. To accomplish the air force mission, elected officials provided the necessary financial resources as the intensity of the Cold War influenced policy making. Since its inception, the air force needed an incredible amount of resources to establish the foundation with which to mitigate Communist threats. The initial outlays were justified; it was either protecting freedom and the nation or losing one's sovereignty and yield to the Soviet empire. The allocation of resources at that moment and throughout the years meant the US Air Force required the best and brightest to maintain optimum operational levels to respond to any threat anywhere in the world. For example, elected officials increased appropriated funding resources steadily, and in the fiscal year 2020, the budget was $184.6 billion.[28] With the increased resources over time, managerial professionalism was critical for oversight to monitor sophisticated budgets,

---

[28] Air Force Magazine, *Journal of the Air Force Association* (June 2020), p. 61.

inventory, maintenance, and training programs. Without the professionalism, the mission would have been compromised, thus posing grave risks to the nation and our allies. Thus, within the air force, the urgency of the mission to use appropriated resources effectively highlighted senior air force leaders' stewardship. In my early days as a young airman, this key aspect of the mission was never really discussed, but should have been. Oversight of resources must be a responsibility of all airmen, regardless of rank.

Professional education. In the US Air Force, training is a serious matter. The professional military is the means by which the air force molds and shapes its personnel to do the air force's way of doing things. Every airman (from the lowest rank to the most senior officers) receives some form of instruction each year to maintain job proficiency, also to get additional background knowledge of something that is of importance to accomplish the mission, and sometimes just to get new emerging information on key aspects of technological advances and leadership techniques. Training should be broadened; however, when something is not effective, it should be modified or removed from the curricula and program. New delivery methods should be considered to save resources and broaden dissemination, but classroom instruction should not be compromised. Classroom instruction is more effective because of the interaction among students and the instructor. And when airmen say that training is not effective, senior leaders must take heed and reevaluate what's needed to change.

Thinking excellence to maintain dominance. Since its founding, standards of excellence produced the world's best airmen (e.g., pilots, maintenance, and logistics experts), which were the top priority of air force senior leaders. The air force training command developed programs with the focus on standards of excellence and the necessity for quality and distinction. For sophisticated equipment, quality and excellence are necessary for all aspects of maintenance. Airmen are expected to do their very best, and with assignments in one's career, this expectation is part of the air force culture. For example, keeping sophisticated systems in their absolute best working conditions is such a common principle that all airmen naturally recognize that is part of their responsibilities. No other thing takes precedence, but that. But it is more than recognition; rather, it is the culture in the organization that training must be accomplished to keep one's proficiency to maintain the highest levels of excellence of readiness to respond to any threat, anywhere in the world. Thinking excellence and applying those of value will shape how things could be done better, to achieve mission success and dominance.

Being the best. Within the air force, there is the expectation that everyone's duty is critical and all airmen must do their absolute best to be the absolute best. This expectation to do one's best comes not only from the vast array of sophisticated resources within the air force inventory and protecting the homeland but also from the US Air Force's mission to protect the country's airspace. Considering the complexity of the technology within air force systems (fighters, planes, missiles, satellites, computers, etc.), there is the belief one cannot afford to tackle one's job in a half-hearted manner. It is the drive to achieve excellence that is expected, and nothing more. This drive, which all airmen are familiar with and which entails all day-to-day activities, is what the air force strives for. The nation expects the air force to accomplish its mission, and in turn, air force senior leaders expect all airmen to excel at everything they do—all airmen know this, and it is indicative of the air force culture, but it will need continued emphasis from senior leaders in appropriate meetings with lower-rank personnel.

Reputation and integrity. One's reputation and integrity are critical personal attributes with which one is continuously judged. In complex organizations or just any organization, one's reputation and integrity must be impeccable. When a fighter pilot steps in a fighter jet, he or she is essentially relying on numerous individuals in the unit and elsewhere for the complete operational readiness of that aircraft. If the pilot were to ask a maintenance airman if all maintenance checks were completed, the pilot would expect an affirmative answer, and nothing else. If the pilot were to get an ambiguous response, the pilot's confidence in the maintenance airman's integrity would immediately be lost. Being cognizant of the need to keep one's reputation and integrity is what is expected throughout the air force, especially for pilots going through their checklist for a mission. Once that reputation is lost, it could be almost impossible to regain it. All airmen must understand this.

The air force family. The air force family—colleagues and friends—is the bedrock foundation for the camaraderie that exists throughout the organization. It is a special bond with current and retired airmen, and it just does not seem to go away. It endures and strengthens with time. By and large, airmen come to see other airmen as family members (as brothers and sisters), either from the initial orientation (basic training) air force training or from professional training, peacetime duty, or combat duty. This bond between airmen permeates throughout the organization. The expectation to treat other airmen with respect builds on the principle that the air force as an institution must be a cohesive organization. The camaraderie seen between other airmen is the fundamental principle for the organizational culture that has evolved in the air force over the years and within which airmen see themselves as part of the air force family. Airmen take friendship and camaraderie sincerely, and thus, every attempt must be taken to make sure such a cordial atmosphere remains a fundamental characteristic of how the air force is known to treat its members.

Quality of life. There is an air force saying commonly known to all airmen that when Congress appropriates money to build an air base, the first things air force senior leaders allocate funds to are the customary, actually, mandatory golf course and officers' and NCO clubs, facilities that are critical to maintaining the US Air Force way of life. This is obviously not true, but airmen take pride in their bases and sometimes would like to believe it is true. Over the years, air force leaders have made it known that quality of life is essential for airmen to maintain positive morale and to be always highly motivated. Quality-of-life programs cost money, and any resources put into these programs reap enormous dividends to keep airmen and their families fit and motivated. For example, it is very common to see at air force bases airmen's enthusiasm to use their fitness and sports facilities with their colleagues, even when not on duty. When in the continental United States or overseas, airmen have come to expect these programs will be available, which have over the years had some degree of consistency at all bases throughout the world. Protecting and expanding quality-of-life programs will pay dividends to provide airmen places to relax, keep fit, and rejuvenate, all critical to achieving a cohesive organization.

In summary, the air force organizational culture provides the foundational values on which airmen perform their duty. From the early days to today, airmen from all walks of life have influenced how rules, guidelines, procedures, and expectations shape airmen. The air force organizational culture, though unwritten, is the tradition and customs on how airmen will conduct themselves and how they will be judged from within and outside the group. The tradition and customs will continue to guide airmen to do extraordinary things on duty. Airmen know what they have to do and will continue to do what is expected of them.

Introspective Thoughts on the Future and Challenges

The future is now for the air force. In this era of accelerated technological advances, thinking of the future as a construct to occur in a few years, or a decade, or even decades should be forever banished from air force reasoning. The new approach should be that technological things are possible; but at what cost, what value, and does the new technology brings efficiency in the defense of the nation?

Senior airmen in leadership positions must widen their thinking aperture. Additionally, they must create an environment to encourage thinking about emerging threats. The incredibly fast pace of new technological advancements and ideas to incorporate into air force systems will require individuals with unconventional opinions. Aircraft, rockets and satellites, and testing equipment will increase in sophistication, with more computer applications, and with incredible capabilities. Recruits will continue to bring incredible technical skills from their civilian experiences but will still need specialized training to operate and maintain equipment to meet air force standards. Further, airmen will need support from every level of the organization to understand the purpose of their respective tasks to be successful in their mission.

The complexities of geopolitical issues will increase. Thus, airmen at all levels must understand and reevaluate their purpose, with respect to achieving their mission. More communication will be needed from top to bottom in an organization and bottom to top for the air force to continue to be effective. Key areas to widen the thinking aperture are as follows:

Thinking strategic. Every airman, regardless of rank, must understand the strategic implications of their respective mission. How each mission is tied to the National Security Strategy (NSS) is important to know. In my earlier days in the air force, strategic implications of what the air force did were very rarely discussed. We did our unit mission because we were told to do it. Junior airmen were not expected to ask questions. But now, asking questions is even more important. Not knowing how a mission is linked to the NSS makes an airman less valuable. The more informed an airman is about the strategic implication of what he or she does, the better it is for the air force, in that the airman becomes more informed about what the commander in chief wants to achieve.

As a lieutenant colonel and, later, as a colonel, issues of strategic implication were common. In these ranks, it was easy to see how a geopolitical issue was important to the United States. Routine discussions with general officers and Department of State officials about operations and engagements tend to revert back to the United States' objectives. But airmen at the major rank and below and NCOs were generally never part of these kinds of discussions. Granted there is a need to know, there is, however, some discretion once an assignment is given to explain strategic implications. Senior leaders must use their discretion. Sharing as much information as possible to junior officers and NCOs about the strategic implication of a task is an early investment to shape an airman for senior roles, and there is no cost associated with this approach.

An environment in which geopolitical issues are discussed, when appropriate, is best for a young airman. He or she will grow in that environment, and when placed in a position that requires such thinking, it will come naturally. Sharing and discussing how a task is linked to NSS will make an airman more intellectually curious to ask questions. Nothing could be more valuable in having a junior airman asking questions in planning an operation, where it is always critical to have alternative viewpoints. The air force will find such informed airmen more valuable and prepared when they are selected for promotion to senior ranks.

Technology. Technological advances for all equipment in the air force inventory have grown exponentially, and the trend is to expect more advances in shorter time spans. Air force senior leaders must be prepared that some advances could become obsolete in months. Research and development and partnership with America's best companies will be critical to ensure that air force keeps its advantage to dominate the airspace with manned and unmanned vehicles.

Recurring replacement of equipment will create chaos in an organization. Prudence in judgment and different perspectives to replace equipment for advanced technology must be considered. For the air force, replacing advanced technology should require deliberation and testing to determine if the new technology warrants acceptance. A change places more stress on an organization in terms of training and usage. If technological capabilities are so complex that senior and midlevel leaders do not understand the full range of capabilities, then younger airmen will be at a loss on when to make decisions. Thus, incorporating new technology must be guided by a range of factors that include prudence, value, and impact of the technology on the mission and airmen. Most of all, risks of the technology to other separate air force systems and limitations must be determined before making a decision to buy. Technology and threats will be two areas that will consume senior leaders' time. And so, a major challenge for air force leaders will be to decide what technology to incorporate and at what cost.

Acquisition. Acquisitions' decisions must be based on making sure the air force has the best equipment for mission success rather than a personal goal to use all allocated funds, to preserve one's budget size for the next year. The process of buying is a critical component of the air force's mission, and reforms must be incorporated to make sure quality goods and services are purchased from reputable vendors for delivery in a reasonable amount of time. To increase efficiency in the process, the air force must continuously review how it conducts business with the private industry and incorporate those practices that are cost-effective and cost-efficient with a goal to buy the best-proven product and not necessarily the lowest bid.

Training. Training will always be a critical component for the air force to maintain its superiority. However, it must continually be reviewed to determine what components to update, broaden, and cancel to ensure effectiveness. Not all airmen at the same rank are equal in capabilities with respect to the technical aspects of the job, and communication skills. Thus, some training must be individually managed at the unit level for some airmen, when possible, rather than on a rank basis to improve their value and broaden their respective perspectives.

Training that is generally reserved only for officers must be opened for qualified NCOs. Opening up new training opportunities for outstanding airmen will benefit the entire system. It will broaden the mind and increase the bond between officers and NCOs and shape individuals to adapt quickly to perform tasks that were never performed before.

Concluding Remarks

Service in the US military is an honorable profession. It is a career that requires individuals with character, integrity, and courage to make decisions to implement the president's national security strategy, which could impact peoples' lives in accomplishing the mission. Duty requires many personal and family sacrifices, and throughout the homeland, there is a high degree of admiration for those who have followed this career path. From the early days of the nation to today, services from average Americans from different regions of the country have established the armed services as an institution that is dedicated and committed to the ideals on which the nation was founded. Throughout the nation, Americans with diverse political ideology still seem to agree that military service has produced individuals with character and integrity. The nation is and will be forever grateful to those who served and who are serving voluntarily and who gave their lives in defense of the nation.

My service in the US Air Force and Reserve component was an enriching experience. Throughout my career, I have had countless opportunities to work on issues that were vital to the United States' national interests in several places in the world. Working alongside exceptional airmen and other members of the Armed Services, I came to believe and even more convinced that service was good for me and that it broadened my perspectives on many, many issues. It was a great learning experience as I interacted with airmen from different backgrounds (from pilots, medical doctors, technicians, and intelligence and policy planners), who projected an enthusiasm about the air force for what they do and what they are required to do. These experiences helped me to be a productive airman. The things I was responsible for and those extraordinary individuals with whom I served shaped my life and my philosophical beliefs about duty, leadership, and success.

The intent of this book was to share some of my experiences during my service. My experiences as I have articulated were frank and represented genuine events that shaped my service career. The air force culture, its philosophy, its mission, and indeed the air force *way of life* were part of the milieu of significant episodes of my life that had the greatest impact on who I am now. Service alongside other airmen doing exceptional things was a regular part of my Air Force Reserve life. As I reflect now and again, my service would not have endured without the help and support from many individuals with whom I have had the privilege to work.

Airmen today have opportunities to work on complex issues of national importance. At every grade level, I have encountered airmen in many parts of the world, and their duty in some little way, while never insignificant, contributed to the overall efforts to protect the US national interests. With service overseas or at a base in the homeland, one's duty is about just another significant sliver in a patchwork of the nation's defense organization. Whether one is aware of this or not, every service member is important to his or her organization. In the air force, everyone fills a critical role, and the whole organization and the nation expect every airman to do his or her very best to serve the nation. From my observations, airmen whether on the flight line, in a maintenance shop, or working on security cooperation issues in the international arena or in a desolate area overseas contribute in their own way to serve the air force and the nation.

It is common today for airmen to serve alongside colleagues from the other branches of the services. Working together with members from the other services was enriching for me. It gave me further insight into the other branches, their mission, and their organizational culture. Whether it was individuals in the Office of the Secretary of Defense, the Joint Staff, or major command, the Department of State, or civilian intelligence agencies, the interactions with other colleagues were insightful. It strengthened my understanding of the national policy making processes and civilian controls over the military. These controls are the bedrock foundation on how the US military was founded and still continue today within the sphere of civilian control. The civilian control will continue to be the most effective oversight to keep the air force an effective fighting force.

Advances in technology (space, computers, Internet, and unmanned aerial vehicles) have given the air force new and broader missions. As a result, the air force has recruited individuals with highly technical skills, mostly young men and women to fill its needs. In this future, the air force will continue to rely on young Americans with such skills. During my time as a colonel, I noticed phenomenal organizational changes within the air force. Specifically, today, you now see young airmen with more responsibilities and working on incredibly complex and sophisticated computer equipment to manage the colossal flow of information between air force bases. Information flow, the lifeblood of all missions, is needed now more than ever to be secure, consistent, and reliable. Airmen (from all ranks) have new responsibilities that directly impact the security of the United States and manage complex systems to make sure air force leaders get the right information in time to make decisions.

My service was extra special opportunities to work alongside leaders from the different service branches. From the Air Intelligence

Agency, to the United States Military Delegation to NATO, to Central Command Headquarters and at Ramstein Air Force Base, I saw effective leaders (military and civilian, to include US ambassadors) in action. These opportunities were the building blocks for my career—they helped me to learn and put into practice successful techniques for leading and getting the mission done. To see general officers (from one to four stars) from the US military and even from other foreign countries in either in international meetings or during negotiations helped to grasp what it takes to be effective. For US general officers in international settings (in which I was in a supporting role), their presence, I believed, shows that military officers must be astute in numerous complex geopolitical issues. More importantly, they must have the communication skills to articulate the United States' positions, clearly, with internal enthusiasm and deep philosophical beliefs, to show what is important for the United States.

For me, serving in the air force was a special privilege. This opportunity to work alongside airmen, marines, sailors, and soldiers presented me with many learning opportunities. To see how other individuals (experienced and less experienced) set about to work on important issues that are vital to the US interests helped me to learn about leadership and what it took to be successful. The attributes for effective leadership and success that I discussed in this book are my own ideas observed throughout my service career and research for my doctoral degree. Throughout my career, I was determined to carry out my air force responsibilities to the best of my ability and within the air force traditions for high standards. I saw how my senior officers managed their work and how they treated me and other colleagues in general. These observations shaped my own philosophical approach to what I wanted to accomplish for the air force. Moreover, the observations were helpful to identify what it takes to be an effective and successful leader.

I have found that the overarching step to be effective and successful is that one must do some introspection and self-analysis. It is through this process that one must be willing to ask oneself the question, "What do I need to do to be an effective and successful leader to accomplish the air force mission?" Just agreeing to do the introspection is a major personal hurdle; for some people, this is impossible to even consider. Once the question is asked and an earnest self-analysis is done to search for answers to problems, one can begin to see what is necessary for the transformation. Next, one must develop a plan of action to do what is necessary to make the personal changes for effective leadership and success. The reflections that I have discussed earlier are straightforward and common sense ideas. I have found in my readings that some scholars, authors, and retired individuals with military experiences have to some extent discussed similar points for effective and successful leaders. Their ideas along with mine would be helpful to those who are sincerely interested in serving their respective branches of service.

As an airman, my service to the air force and the reserve was always voluntary. It was an honor to work alongside dedicated airmen, marines, soldiers, and sailors from different backgrounds, and I have found that despite long hours, the work was indeed rewarding, and I learned from each of them. Knowing that somehow, I contributed in some way a small part to the air force mission, alongside unpretentious airmen, was satisfying and rewarding.

For current and future airmen, the air force mission will continue to change to face incredible and unforeseen threats. The air force will forever have a need for patriotic and dedicated individuals to defend the homeland and the US interests overseas. And with the new Space Command comes new opportunities, challenges, and threats. But the fundamental human element of the mission will be the same, and that is each airman must be ready, at a moment's notice, to go anywhere in the world or beyond to defend freedom as a volunteer, without any expectation for recognition or award.

That spirit, the American spirit of curiosity of what is over the hill, will continue in the best traditions and heritage of the air force and the nation's courageous aviators. And thus, the air force must continue to nurture the professional growth and human needs of all its personnel. And with the end of one's service comes the honor of being a veteran and the joy of having fellow airmen, other US servicemen, and international military personnel as sincere friends for life.

ABOUT THE AUTHOR

In the early 1970s, America was in turmoil over the war in Vietnam, and many male college students were worried about going to Vietnam; Marty was one of those. With a low draft number, he reported for his aptitude tests, but President Richard Nixon ended the draft on January 27, 1973, thus terminating the need for draftees. In January 1976, Marty enlisted in the United States Air Force, and after finishing college part-time, he earned his commission on July 31, 1987. He trained as an intelligence officer and worked with the Air Intelligence Agency, US Mission to NATO, the US Military Delegation to NATO, and the US Mission to the European Union in Brussels, Central Command, in Tampa, Florida, and the US Air Forces Europe and Africa at Ramstein Air Force Base in Germany. His assignments took him to Armenia, Azerbaijan, Belgium, The Republic of Georgia, Germany, Greece, Korea, India, Pakistan, Qatar, and Turkey. He worked side-by-side with marines, soldiers, sailors, coastguardsmen, US diplomats, and international officers. Marty worked on security cooperation and intelligence sharing programs. He is a graduate of the US Air War College in-residence program and has a doctorate from the University of North Florida, a master's degree from Troy State, and a bachelor's degree from Hunter College. Col. Khan's story, *Uncommon Duties in the United States Air Force*, highlights the value of service to the nation, attributes for effective leaders, and looks ahead at the challenges for the US Air Force. Col. Khan retired in February 2015.